Of a Place and a Time

Richard D. Altick

Of a Place and a Time

Remembering Lancaster

Archon 1991

Printed in the United States of America

The paper used in this publication meets the
minimum requirements of American National Standard
for Information Sciences—Permanence of Paper for
Printed Library Materials, ANSI Z39.48—1984. ∞

Library of Congress Cataloging-in-Publication Data

Altick, Richard Daniel, 1915–
Of a place and a time : remembering Lancaster
Richard D. Altick.
p.   cm.
1. Lancaster (Pa.)—Social life
and customs.   2. Pennsylvania Dutch—Pennsylvania
—Lancaster—Social life and customs.
3. Altick, Richard Daniel, 1915–   —Childhood and youth.
4. Lancaster (Pa.)—Biography.   I. Title.
F159.L2A45   1991   90-29296
974.8'15—dc20
ISBN 0-208-02321-6

CONTENTS

v

Author's Note

This is an informal memoir of a small eastern city, Lancaster, Pennsylvania, as I knew it between the two world wars. To its longtime inhabitants, every city has a personality of its own, even though much may lie in the subjective sensibility of the beholder. Gertrude Stein once complained of Oakland, California, that there was no *there* there. In Lancaster, as I grew up, I sensed plenty of thereness, and the following pages are the result of my effort to capture and convey what that intangible quality consisted of.

After having spent my whole adult life in a profession that values historical accuracy as a pearl of great price, I have allowed myself, this time, the licentious luxury of not pausing to look anything up in books. My "facts" may be wrong once in a while but, to use the phrase I heard over and over again when I attended criminal trials in the Lancaster County courthouse, this is the way it was "to the best of my recollection." Unlike those material witnesses, I am, happily, not under oath.

In the same relaxed spirit, I have allowed myself to write of "the Pennsylvania Dutch," though I know very well that the "proper" (pedantic?) term is "Pennsylvania German." "Dutch" is the universally used popular name, and in addition is the older word: at the time Pennsylvania was first settled, Germans were, and for centuries had been, commonly called Dutch. So the latter has the authority of history behind it.

To preserve the reminiscential mode intact, I have written in the past tense throughout. Often, if the reader wishes, the past tense may be transposed to the present: though much that I write about is gone, much remains; many of the places and habits described still exist. In the last pages of the epilogue, certain observations that I have couched, for consistency's sake, in the narrative past tense might equally well have been written in the descriptive present, for a regrettable reason that will be clear at that point.

R.D.A.

THE PLACE, THE TIMES

A number of years ago, on a narrow-gauge Alpine train cautiously snaking its way down from Zermatt, I fell into conversation with a Swiss woman who, it transpired, had just come back from a visit to her daughter and son-in-law in Washington, D.C. I asked the (to me) inevitable question: what sight, of those in the eastern United States she had been taken to see, interested her most? Her answer was unexpected. It was the Pennsylvania Dutch country centering in Lancaster County, Pennsylvania.

The irony struck me. Admittedly, she had more reason than most foreign tourists in the United States to be interested in the Pennsylvania Dutch. Though I suppose she didn't see it that way, she had made a pious pilgrimage in the form of a sightseeing tour. Some of the Pennsylvania Dutch whose meticulously cultivated farms she saw might have been among her forebears had they not emigrated to the New World in the first half of the eighteenth century, for most of them came from the valleys of Switzerland and the Rhineland. The family names she would have seen on signs in the Lancaster farmers' markets—Huber, Hess, Wenger, Nissley—include names that are lettered on the stalls that today are set up, twice a week, along the Reuss River in the center of Lucerne by the farmers and truck gardeners of the region. Among these, however, are no longer any Amish or Mennonites, the splinter groups who fled from the wars, political upheavals, and religious persecutions that had racked their homeland for as long as anyone could remember. To see the "plain people" in the costumes they wore two centuries ago and still wear today, as with great difficulty they pursue a way of life detached from worldly vanities, one has to travel to southeastern Pennsylvania, to what amounts to a living museum spread over many square miles, the past encapsulated in the midst of onrushing late twentieth-century America.

Had there been occasion to do so, I might have described to my Swiss acquaintance my very different image of Lancaster, not so much the county but the moderate-sized city that was its seat. In long retrospect, the anomaly, the paradox, is sharper than it was when I was growing up, absorbing the manifold impressions that my memory persists in retaining. Spending one's childhood and youth in Lancaster city was quite different from spending it in the surrounding countryside. Life in town contained nothing out of the ordinary then. In many significant respects, Lancaster could have served as well as Muncie, Indiana, for the model of the "typical" small American city that Robert and Helen Lynd called

2

Middletown in their classic sociological profile. But in spite of that typicality, it was never chosen as a test market for any new consumer products: its demography was too askew to represent a true cross section of urban America. To grow up in Lancaster therefore was not like growing up in any other American city or town. Its ordinariness was not that of the Brooklyn, New York, that Alfred Kazin described in *Walker in the City*, or that of H.L. Mencken's Baltimore, Thomas Wolfe's Asheville, Sherwood Anderson's Winesburg, Ohio, or Sinclair Lewis's Sauk Center.

To its inhabitants such as my young self, jumping the delivery trucks of the city's leading department store, pumping gas for Gulf Refining, reading self-composed commercial spots before a microphone at the town's only radio station, Lancaster had all the feel of the American modernity of the period, F. Scott Fitzgerald's as well as Mencken's and Lewis's. Yet, as the local booster literature never failed to point out, it had an important past. Time marched on, as the portentous-voiced announcer in the newsreels and on the radio proclaimed ("Time"—pause—"marches on!"), but time also stood still, not least in the rural Amish-Mennonite areas where the past was preserved in the routine of everyday life.

Furthermore, Lancaster's geographical location differentiated it from many otherwise comparable communities. It was, and probably always had been, even in the days of slow transportation and communication, both independent and dependent. As the county seat, the city was the planet around which such satellite country towns

3

as Ephrata, Columbia, Quarryville, Lititz, Manheim, and Elizabethtown revolved; but this miniature system was, in turn, fixed in the greater orbit of Philadelphia, which influenced much that Lancaster, the city, thought and did.

By sheer accident, the farther and nearer time-brackets of my evocation of a Lancaster past are located in the same place, Buchanan Park, the only public park of any size within the city limits, a many-acred expanse of greensward and playing fields in the northwest quadrant, faced by substantial middle-class homes that sat behind well-kept lawns along Buchanan Avenue and Race Avenue. In the summer of 1918, a Liberty Bond rally was held there. A replica of the little, long since vanished city hall downtown, where the Continental Congress met for a single day in 1777 as it fled British-occupied Philadelphia on its way to the embattled colonies' less temporary capital in York, thirty miles farther west, was built for the occasion. But of supreme interest was a state-of-the-aviation-art biplane, which had landed on the grass and was available for close inspection. This, I think, is my earliest memory of Lancaster.

The biplane soared off to promote bond sales elsewhere, but the little yellow and white building remained, a permanent landmark that was eventually turned into a storage shed for park equipment. So did a slope that remained from the days when a small earthen reservoir had been dug to boost water pressure in the West End. Having burst the first time it was filled, by 1918 it had been replaced by a tall steel tank with a pinched-in cone for a tower, which later was joined by a second, larger one whose size and shape suggested it had been transplanted from one of the oil refineries along the Delaware downstream from Philadelphia. The slope's angle was gentle enough to require some determination on the part of kids who wanted to roll down it in summer—thus inducing early skepticism about Newton's law of gravity—but steep enough to make it a favorite sledding hill in winter, broader than several streets and with no traffic to worry about.

In December 1941, Buchanan Park suddenly became a military target, thanks to those big tanks on the border between the park and the campus of Franklin and Marshall College to the east. If they were sabotaged, water would cease to flow from the kitchen faucets of a large portion of the West End. And so a sentry box was hastily erected and there, night after night, with only an oil lantern for illumination—and no means of communication with the local civil defense HQ, so far as a passerby could tell—patiently sat one or another of a cadre of old men, like the napping "watch" or "Charlies" who theoretically maintained the nocturnal peace of pre-Dickensian London. The saboteurs never came, and I don't know how the old man on lonely duty would have dealt with them if they had. Lancaster, in this respect, was as unprepared for the enemy as England had been a year or two earlier when its home guard drilled with wooden rifles.

The Second World War had little visible effect on

5

Lancaster County. No big matériel factories were built, and the local contribution to the war effort was made within existing facilities. The Hamilton Watch Company, for example, made chronometers and fuzes for the Navy, and the Sensenig brothers' small plant out in the country carved propellers for aircraft. No one anticipated the transformation the countryside was fated to undergo in the post-war years. In the 1920s and 1930s it remained what it had always been: a rich farming county with red-brown earth, not as flat as Indiana nor quite as "gently rolling" as the Chamber of Commerce described it, with clumps of woods here and there, and narrow macadam-ized roads winding past gray fieldstone farmhouses, odorous red barns, and tobacco-curing sheds with slat-ted vertical vents. Once in a while the road might pass an old water-driven grist mill and make a sharp turn to cross the stream on a one-lane covered bridge floored with loose planks that clattered under a car's wheels.

This prosperous, tranquil showplace of rural America was enclosed within the pentagon of Lancaster County, whose base rested securely on the Mason-Dixon line, as the Pennsylvania-Maryland border, the dividing line between the nation's North and South, was called. To the west, the boundary was defined by the shallow, almost mile-wide Susquehanna River, flowing between low hills as it neared the end of its silt-laden course from the "coal regions" upstate to the Chesapeake Bay. Between Lancaster and York County, on the far shore, there was, in 1918, only a one-track iron railroad bridge from Columbia, on the eastern shore, to Wrightsville on the western. Such small motor traffic as there was as yet had to await the convenience of this branch of the Pennsylvania Railroad; between trains, people drove their Fords across on the planked roadway. This arrangement became increasingly intolerable as more cars—Chevvies, Essexes, Reos, Dodges, Hudsons—hit the roads, and sometime in the 1930s a highway bridge was built alongside the one that had caused all the bottlenecks. It was a great day when motorists were liberated from the tyranny of slow-moving freights.

A short distance below Three Mile Island, which was to become world-famous in a later era, the Lancaster County line left the Susquehanna and struck eastward, along the borders first of Dauphin County (site of Harrisburg, the state capital), then of Lebanon County, then of Berks. The names reflected the mixed origins of the early settlers. The name Dauphin, referring to the eldest son of a French king, was one of the few links southeastern Pennsylvania had with France; apart from a scattering of Huguenot émigrés, some of whom settled in Lancaster County and left such names as Lefever, Bushong, and Ferree, the French were noticeably missing from the spectrum of nationalities who colonized the area.

The hills on the Lebanon and Berks borders once contained large deposits of iron. At Cornwall as late as the 1930s, the Bethlehem Steel Company operated a deep open-pit mine—an incongruous Mesabi in Pennsylvania Dutch land. There was even a row of rundown brownstone company houses across the road. Farther to the east were the Welsh Mountains, which actually were no more than high, densely wooded hills. Here, primitive ironworks and forges had once fashioned the extracted ore into arms for Washington's army, including the well-made "Pennsylvania rifle." An outpost of Appalachia, this relatively wild territory was home to poor whites who came to the attention of Lancastrians only when their moonshining, horse-stealing, and homicides stemming from their family feuding came to the attention of the state police and, subsequently, the Lancaster County courts. The notorious, indeed half-legendary Abe Buzzard and his extended family, constantly in and out of jail, were the closest that sedate Lancaster came to having a native criminal tradition. Today the Pennsylvania Turnpike slices through their old fiefdom.

The Welsh had not been among the most numerous settlers of this part of the country. They left many more place names—Llanerch, Tredyffrin, Bryn Mawr, Bala Cynwyd—in the outskirts of Philadelphia; in Lancaster County, only Caernarvon, Lampeter, and Brecknock preserved their memory. But they contributed to the diversified local nomenclature that qualified the assumption that Lancaster had always been, first and foremost, Pennsylvania Dutch territory. Apart from New Holland, Manheim, and Strasburg, there was no direct evidence that the settlers had come from any particular part of Europe. Their origins were suggested indirectly by the many family names that were bestowed on the little towns: Neffsville, Brickerville, Reinholds, Brunnerville, Hinkletown, Rothsville, Bowmanville, Reamstown, Rohrerstown, Millersville, Landisville, Kinzer; but there

THE PLACE, THE TIMES

were also Elizabethtown, Brownstown, and Adamstown, which were not necessarily Germanic. A few names reflected religious influence, Ephrata and Mount Nebo; others were borrowed from the Indians, Pequea (pronounced "peckway"), Salunga, Cocalico, Conestoga; some were descriptive, Quarryville and Gap (in the low hills on the Lancaster-Chester County border). Several, Blue Ball, White Horse, Bird in Hand, and Compass, derived from the signs at old taverns. And finally, there were the names that bespoke the presence of appreciative or hopeful settlers and land salesmen: New Providence, Fruitville, Mount Joy, Paradise, Eden.

Such was the lay of the land, except that I have omitted what was in some ways its most significant feature. On the east, Lancaster adjoined Chester County; beyond Chester County lay Montgomery and Delaware Counties; and then one was in Philadelphia. While it could hardly be said that from Lancaster all roads led to Philadelphia, it was a fact that most movement, from the earliest days, was west-east, with stress on the latter. The wide Susquehanna, bridged at only one place, served as a psychological barrier orienting Lancaster toward the Philadelphian east rather than the Yorkist west. Baltimore and Washington, to be sure, lay not much farther to the south, but their felt presence was negligible, especially since they were not connected with Lancaster by major transportation routes such as the two that bisected the county and led directly to Philadelphia, only seventy miles away.

One was the Philadelphia Pike, as it was called locally.

It was the Lancaster-Philadelphia segment of the Lincoln Highway (later, US 30), the first integrated route from coast to coast, and the one that carried settlers' wagon trains westward from Lancaster, an important equipping and staging point, to the Allegheny Mountains, and thence to the frontier. In modern times, running through the center of Lancaster city on King Street, it bore most of the state's east-west traffic and thus brought the dubious blessing of heavy trucks and intercity buses to the downtown area. No bypass was even contemplated then, and the only solution to the problem was the easy, but eventually inadequate, one of making King Street eastbound only and Orange, the next north, westbound.

Out in the county, along the Lincoln Highway, the first evidences appeared of roadside commercial development, gas stations, drive-in movies, food stands, and primitive motels, which were often no more than rows of detached small frame cabins with gravel driveways. (In towns along the way as well as in Lancaster itself, private homes in those pre-bed-and-breakfast days hung out shingles advertising "tourist rooms.") There was even a tourist-trap wolf farm, actually an exhibition of caged wolves, near the Chester County line. Most of the highway was two-lane, but in its eastern stretch a third lane was added. Bloody experience soon taught that devoting the middle of a highway to a two-way passing lane was not a good idea; the road in the vicinity of Gap Hill became known as "Death Highway," and it may have contributed to the stock of the unlovely automobile graveyards that sprang up in the county, along with a plethora of billboards.

The second route to Philadelphia was the main line (Chicago to New York) of the Pennsylvania Railroad, affectionately known as the "Pennsy," a brave four-lane iron highway which, until the internal combustion engine took away most of the passenger trains in the 1950s, was Lancaster's chief link with the civilization farther east. By the best trains, which stopped only at Paoli, the western gateway to the rich Philadelphia suburbs that collectively were named for the railroad ("the Main Line," capitalized), Broad Street Station, in the heart of the city, was hardly more than seventy minutes away. New York City was no more than double that, or so it seemed. It was no trick at all for Lancaster women over a certain income level to go to Philadelphia for a day's shopping, perhaps to meet friends at the great golden eagle in the square atrium of John Wanamaker's department store. Buyers from Lancaster dress shops could even make day trips to their New York suppliers, though they had to leave early in the morning. The return trip in the evening was less taxing if, in post-Prohibition days, the train carried a bar-equipped club car.

The availability of the Pennsy's fast trains could make a crucial difference in one's life. I could commute to graduate classes at the University of Pennsylvania, returning to Lancaster in the early evening by what seemed to be, whether it was or not, the fastest train in the system, the Susquehannock, which was headed for Harrisburg and went from there up the Susquehanna to

11

Williamsport. It was not much of a train, consisting merely of an early model electric locomotive, a baggage car, two coaches, and, inexplicably, a milk car hooked to the rear, but it tore along at better than a mile a minute, slowing only to negotiate the Gap curve west of Coatesville.

Only the Pennsylvania's premier train, the all-Pullman Broadway Limited, failed to pause at Lancaster. Its string of sleepers, diner, and club car, painted in the PRR's distinctive Tuscan red, thundered through the station on the inside tracks without even condescending to slow down. On bitter winter mornings, as one waited for the eastbound Red Arrow from Detroit, the Broadway would pass through, its cars coated with ice, men in their undershirts interrupting their shaving to wipe the window clear of frost to see where they were. (Lancaster, Pa., and you're running thirty minutes late; but perhaps this was the Limited's second section. In those days second sections were sometimes required on the most popular trains at peak seasons.)

The main line, grazing the city's northern limits, was called the cutoff, to distinguish it from the loop it had once dropped down to an ancient station at Queen and Chestnut Streets, only two blocks from Lancaster's central intersection and across the street from the best hotel, the Brunswick. The depot—the better term, considering the station's age—had a gloomy waiting room and a sooty, barrel-roofed train shed, and it was an intolerable barrier to progress. The trains belched smoke and made noise, and, what was worst, they

12

draped themselves across busy North Queen Street. This became a civic issue of no small moment. The Brunswick Hotel hung out a banner that could be seen by every passenger as a train waited: DON'T JUDGE OUR CITY BY OUR RAILROAD STATION.

Finally, about 1929, the railroad capitulated. It tore down the depot, replacing one eyesore with another, a parking lot that was to endure there for half a century, and snipped the loop that reached from the cutoff, leaving vestigial trackage that rusted away from disuse. But in the open fields along the cutoff, at the end of North Duke Street, the company built a showplace of a station, complete with a whole row of ticket windows, a restaurant, an ample waiting room, and a broad over-pass, a concourse really, giving access to the platforms. If the spacious new building was not actually walled and floored with marble, that was the impression it gave. The long, roofed platforms, each serving two tracks, could accommodate the longest trains. Theoretically it was possible for Lancaster to handle four of the Pennsy's fliers—the Broadway Limited, the Spirit of St. Louis (named for Lindbergh's transatlantic plane), the Jeffersonian, and the Red Arrow (from Detroit) at one time. This was a remote contingency, but the mere thought that Lancaster was prepared for it did wonders for local pride. The opening of the station and the accompanying electrification of the line, even if it meant the retirement of the steam locomotives, those powerful, high-wheeled black beauties bearing on their front the road's red keystone emblem, were among the proudest events in Lancaster's history.

The city the railroad served was laid out as early as 1730, not by German immigrants but by pioneers of another strain, Scotch-Irish settlers named Hamilton. Its original square form and dimensions, two miles on a side, endured for more than two centuries, until its northern side was bulged out to annex the tax-rich factory property of Armstrong Cork. Following the precedent of William Penn in Philadelphia, its streets were plotted on the gridiron pattern which no natural barriers interrupted: the Conestoga Creek, which lent its name to the locally made prairie wagons (as they would be called in the next century), meandered on its way from the Welsh Mountains to the Susquehanna some distance from the city's eastern limits, and the only protuberance within the boundaries, called Cabbage Hill because of its sauerkraut-making German population, was not much as hills went, even in southeastern Pennsylvania. The two axis streets, neatly dividing the city into quadrants, were King and Queen. Queen was paralleled by Prince on the west and Duke on the east (there was no Princess or Duchess). Orange Street, north of King, probably was not named for the Dutch nobility of that name in William Penn's time, even though it had supplied William of Orange to the English throne. It was one of the many botanical, especially arboreal, street names that were fashionable in eighteenth-century

America: Vine, Lemon, Plum, Lime, Walnut, Chestnut, Mulberry, Locust, Strawberry, Spruce, Elm, Pine.

At the junction of King and Queen Streets was the Square, the heart of the business district. More formally, it was known as both Penn Square and Center Square, again in emulation of Philadelphia, which, however, had four other squares equidistant from the central one. Lancaster had only one, and it was not much of a square, as American, and particularly Philadelphian, squares went. In its middle was a hideous Civil War monument in the shape of a granite obelisk inscribed with the names of battles in which Lancastrians had fought—Antietam, Chancellorsville, Chickamauga, Bull Run, Shiloh, Gettysburg, Vicksburg, Chattanooga—and at each corner was a statue, heroic in posture and armament, of a representative soldier or sailor. What with the local and Lincoln Highway through traffic that had to be channeled around the monument, and the streetcar tracks and loading zones that curved around all four sides, it was periodically proposed for removal. But surviving Civil War veterans, though their ranks were steadily thinning, and sentimental pressure from their families managed to keep the monument just where it was. The Square, in fact, was a perennial headache to the people who wanted to keep things moving. When East King Street was made one way east, the automobile traffic had to buck the trolleys in the middle of the street, which were heading west to their terminal in the Square. This was a very undesirable arrangement, but it lasted until the streetcars finally gave way to buses in the late 1930s.

Some of the residential streets were lined with shade trees, which were vulnerable to age and disease; when they had to be cut down, they were often not replaced. The streets were also narrow. In fact, when a railroad spur still ran down the middle of one downtown street, a shifting engine could not pull its one or two cars through if carelessly parked automobiles protruded too far from the curb. There were only two wide thoroughfares in the whole of the city, and these were President Avenue, out beyond Buchanan Park, and West End Avenue, which ran from the Millersville Pike to the park. They had grass plots and clumps of evergreen trees in the middle, barely leaving space for one line of parked cars and another of moving traffic. Indifferent to the dignity of boulevards, Lancastrians were as uninterested as most town dwellers of the time in the amenities of urban planning, and there was little interest, likewise, in zoning and building restrictions.

The city's four square miles were compactly settled. Most of the in-town residential building I remember consisted of filling up such scattered vacant lots as then existed. The home-building thrust was mostly to the west, beyond the city limits, where the Woodlawn development and later, in the 1930s, the poshest of Lancaster's residential areas, School Lane Hills, were built, from Wheatland Avenue northward. Grandview Heights, slightly inferior to these in social prestige, sprang up north of the city, beyond the railroad cutoff. (The hills in the one case and the heights in the other were pure figments of the developer's imagination.) At the same time, there was a certain amount of ribbon building along the roads leading out of the city, the Columbia, Millersville, Lititz, Manheim, Oregon, New Holland, and Philadelphia Pikes among them. ("Pike" was the local generic term, deriving from the fact that some roads had been built as toll roads or turnpikes. I remember the toll house on the Marietta Pike near the city limits, long disused as such but still serving as a dwelling.)

The predominant characteristic of Lancaster houses, as was true in some other Pennsylvania Dutch towns, was their standing in unbroken rows, sometimes from one end of a block to the other. They were built of local red brick, with slate roofs from which poked the dormer windows of the attic. The gradations of size and style represented a clear social hierarchy. The cheapest class clung to the basic design: front walls built flush with the sidewalk (often brick, though replaced by concrete when repairs were made), with three or four concrete steps leading up to the front door. A superior type, perhaps the majority, were recessed from the sidewalk sufficiently to allow a tiny patch of lawn, and the continuous-row pattern was modified to the extent that the houses, though still identical, were paired, a passageway between each pair leading to a back yard divided from its neighbors by whitewashed fences and giving access to a rear alley. The top-drawer row houses, found, for instance, in the vicinity of the College and Buchanan Avenue intersection, was distinguished by stone trimmings and generally larger dimensions, with a finished third floor instead of an attic.

17

Most middle- and upper-grade houses had front porches with their wicker chairs and swinging chain-hung settees, a summer necessity when home air conditioning was undreamed of. All of which—the common walls, the porches lined up in a long row—produced an atmosphere of neighborliness that was slightly diminished in neighborhoods where individually designed houses were set apart from the adjoining ones. Fully detached houses, with ornamental iron railings along the sidewalk, larger lawns at front and side, and trees in the back yard lined some of the "better" streets such as West Chestnut and the westward reaches of Marietta Avenue. Many were entered from the porch by way of a vestibule leading in turn to the house proper. No vestibule, which served in winter as a buffer between the cold outside and the heated house, was complete without a ceramic umbrella stand. It was also the place where you parked your wet rubbers or galoshes.

The Keiper house on North Duke Street was one of only two homes inside the city limits to occupy the better part of a block, and it was widely regarded as being unacceptably ostentatious, not least because it included a large glassed-in conservatory. Until School Lane Hills was built on the outskirts, with its winding streets, oversize lots, and expensive houses, the most affluent families tended to build along one of the roads radiating out from the city, especially to the west and north. Their homes, set well back from the road, with an acre or two of well-maintained lawns and gardens, were the nearest Lancaster came to domestic display, and these, compared with the great estates along Philadelphia's Main Line from Merion to Paoli, were modest indeed. Mansions did not fit in with the Lancaster way of life. Neither did examples of futuristic architecture. On President Avenue, some resolutely deviant property owner built a house with a distinct, indeed blatant, flavor of Frank Lloyd Wright. It was locally derided as "the streamlined garbage can" and it remained the unique example of modernist style in Lancaster.

Seen from a distance, the city was far from possessing a high profile. The only building of any height was the dozen-storied Griest Building on the northwest corner of the Square, owned by the power company and named for its president, who had served several terms in Congress. When the Fuller Construction Company, *of New York City*, no less, dug a big excavation for it, Lancaster was torn between pride—at last, a metropolis!—and depreciation: this, a *skyscraper*? But, lacking any competition except from the Buchanan Park water towers and the Armstrong linoleum plant half a mile north of them, this square, stubby building was to Lancaster what the Eiffel Tower was to Paris or the dome of St. Paul's Cathedral to London.

Closer in, the skyline was marked by a number of church steeples and water tanks stilted on factory and warehouse roofs, such as were depicted at the time by Charles Demuth, a son of the Demuths (locally pronounced DEEmuth), who owned a tobacco shop on East King Street. His celebrity in the art world of the day went unnoticed in his native city.

19

Few buildings exceeded four stories. This was the commanding height of the two leading department stores, Watt and Shand ("Wattnshand" on Lancaster tongues) and Hager's, and most of the other stores along North Queen Street. The Woolworth Building was something special; it antedated by some years the famous Gothic skyscraper of the same name in New York City. Lacking its future namesake's exuberant ornamentation, it was an undistinguished six-story structure, half a block deep, with a model five-and-ten-cent store on the ground floor and a variety of offices—stockbrokers', insurance and real estate agents', chiropodists' and dentists'—above. On top was once a roof garden for summer entertainments, remotely akin to the one atop Madison Square Garden where the architect Stanford White was shot and killed by Harry K. Thaw, jealous of White's attentions to his showgirl wife, Evelyn Nesbit. But both roof gardens were before my time; they were typical of the Theodore Roosevelt era rather than that of Woodrow Wilson.

I did, however, have something of a personal interest in Lancaster's Woolworth Building, because F.W. Woolworth had erected it as a token of gratitude to the city where he had his first success. In 1879, his pioneer nothing-above-ten-cents store in Utica, New York, having just gone bankrupt, he came to Lancaster to start over again. According to a family tradition, which I may well have invented, he bought out my maternal grandfather, whose racket (variety) store was in a bad way. My grandfather no doubt rubbed his hands with satisfaction

over having unloaded the doomed business; it was not
his concern that the purchaser's track record contained
no evidence that he would make a go of it. But Woolworth
did, and from what had been the decaying stump of my
grandfather's business burgeoned Woolworth's five-and-
dime empire. Only in recent years, being of an over-
curious mind, have I discovered that the dates don't fit.
I have therefore, with some regret, withdrawn the story
from circulation.

Binding the city-county community together, in years
before most Lancastrians owned a car, let alone the two
in every garage promised by the Republican campaign in
1928, was the trolley system, which was an inextricable
part of the urban ambience in the 1920s, in Lancaster
as elsewhere. "Inextricable" even in a literal sense,
because the car tracks were so tightly embedded in the
brick or asphalt roadway that it would have been a major
undertaking to rip them up when buses finally took over;
most of the time, they were simply covered with asphalt,
and their removal had to await the complete reconstruction of the street. The very presence of those tracks
added to the air of permanence that characterized every
town like Lancaster. In a subtle way, the fixedness of the
tracks communicated itself to the neighborhood. Streetcar routes could not easily be changed, whereas bus lines
could be rerouted whenever it was expedient to do so.
Thus, the bright yellow trolleys of the Conestoga Trac-
tion Company were embedded not only in the streets
but, figuratively speaking, in the Lancastrian way of life.

In addition to being the chief means by which people got around, they even marked time. Entry after entry in my mother's diary, kept in the early years of the century, noted that "Aunt Ella came out on the 3 o'clock Columbia car" or "Mrs. Edwards missed the 2:20 Marietta Avenue."

Because the streets were too narrow to accommodate two sets of tracks, all the city lines were of the single-track belt variety, some taking circuitous routes before returning to their common place of origin, one of the four curves around the monument in the Square. Suburban lines, as they were called—Lancaster did not have any true interurbans, as other parts of the country did—used the belt tracks inside town. From the Square cars headed out in all directions, Quarryville, Millersville (with an obscure, seldom-operated extension to Pequea on the Susquehanna: riding it, as I once did, had the adventurous flavor of an African expedition), Columbia, Elizabethtown, Manheim, Lititz, Adamstown. One route even crossed the Chester County border on its way to the steel mill town of Coatesville. From the end of several of these lines the cars of other companies took passengers on to Harrisburg, Hershey, Lebanon, and Reading. At one time it was possible, with two changes, to ride trolleys all the way from Lancaster to the 69th Street terminus in Philadelphia. On special occasions such as a big parade or a store or church picnic, cars of different makes from other cities, in their exotic plumage of red, green, or cream, could be seen mingling with the canaries on the Conestoga tracks, as arresting a sight as would

22

have been a flotilla of Chinese junks sailing up the unpicturesque Susquehanna.

I write with authority about all this because at a very early age I contracted a trolley car fixation that was never wholly cured; it has persisted into an era when streetcars have re-emerged as "light rail vehicles." While other kids were obsessed with aviation (I saw such a one at my fiftieth high school reunion, and he was as fixated as ever) or with the stars and standings of major league baseball teams, I poured my observant and imaginative faculties, not to say my passionate attachment, into streetcars. For six cents and a free transfer I could ride on two city lines, raptly absorbing every minute detail of a car's operation, beginning when I paid my fare. The conductor rang up the six cents by rotating an overhead rod to the Ohmer register at the end of the car to show "6¢." He then pulled a cord—one of two suspended from the ceiling, the other being used to signal the motorman, *ding* to stop, *ding-ding* to go—and the transaction was thereby completed and put on record. (Long before this, registers had been introduced to keep the conductors honest.) I admired, and desired, the metal money changer on the conductor's belt.

The oldest trolleys in Conestoga service in the 1920s had hinged rope-net cowcatchers that were lowered toward the track in front. Because there were no turnaround loops at the end of the suburban lines, before beginning the trip back to town the motorman had to hitch up the (former) front cowcatcher and lower the (former) rear one and similarly reverse the trolley poles.

23

I watched these maneuvers with the same close attention I exercised when I rode right behind the motorman on the front bench of the open-air summer cars, watching him vigorously cranking the brass handbrake handle, these cars being unequipped with air brakes.

One operation remained a mystery to me for years. When a car came to a branching switch, how did it know which direction to take? The explanation that satisfied me, much longer than it should have been acceptable to anybody with a dawning intelligence, was that the motorman was capable of telepathy, and that by merely *thinking* which way he wanted to turn at the next corner he could communicate his will to the switch. Only after my powers of ratiocination had reached normal proportions did it occur to me that, perched on the overhead wire, fifty feet or so ahead of a switch was a little circuit box, and that when the switch was already set correctly, the motorman threw off his power and coasted past the box. When he wanted to move the switch, he went past the box with the power on, thus tripping it. If he forgot, he would swear under his breath, stop the car, get out with the crowbar kept for such a contingency, and pry the switch by hand. (Two or three years ago, only a few yards from the Opernring in Vienna, I saw a vexed motorman wielding the crowbar, and more than sixty years fell from my shoulders in an instant.)

Trolleys were an indispensable part of my animate world. Each type of Conestoga car had its own special character, beginning with its voice: the ones that operated in the city had only bells for the motorman's foot to clang, but the older types of suburban cars had shrill whistles, and the newer, heavier models had a bass-baritone tessitura—*Boooooooop-booooop, boop-boop*. Destination signs on the older cars were square metal sheets that fitted into grooves on the front: E for Ephrata, L/F for Laurel and Filbert, W/B for West Belt, M/A for Marietta Avenue, 7/W for Seventh Ward, K for Kinzer. Later models had roll-up fabric scrolls, spelling out destinations, above the front window.

The open cars that ran in summer, the ones that were mounted on a single truck and as a consequence rocked and danced skittishly as they coasted down a hill, were gay and frivolous, as did not become their age, which was considerable even in the 1920s. Their big brothers, broad open cars that came out of the barn on summer Saturdays, Sundays, and holidays to haul the crowds to the amusement parks, or that were pressed into service for big picnics, struck me, despite their festive function, as being the embodiments of settled sobriety, like bank presidents. They probably seated three times as many people as did the other kind, and they seemed to be conscious of their magnified responsibility. (These were the kind that had benches straight across, with drop curtains in case of rain, and running boards along which the fare-collecting conductor scrambled, hand over hand, like a simian church usher.)

Each kind of closed car had its own personality, too. The ones used for many years on the Columbia line, their roofs gently curved fore and aft, struck me as being distinguished for solidity and stability of character. For the little Birney one-man cars that eventually took over all the city lines nobody had much good to say. They were called "blunderbuses" or, in allusion to a popular newspaper cartoon series by Fontaine Fox, Toonerville trolleys. But all were, in my imagination, alive, and if one was disabled by some mechanical failure and its trolley pole was pulled down from the wire and fixed under a roof bracket, I sensed that something was wrong, as if a person was stricken with a mild paralysis. It was worse to see a car, its front bashed in by an accident, being towed to the barn by the seldom-seen wrecking car: I had to avert my eyes from my grievously injured friend.

Most of the motormen and conductors had their regular routes and became part of the familiar neighborhood scene. Some of the old-timers in fact went around the same belt line—a complete circuit might take half an hour—for twenty years. On a one-man car, the motorman sat on his hard stool all day long, running the car, clanging the foot bell in traffic, opening and shutting the folding doors, making change, ringing up fares, and being quietly hospitable to his customers.

For a year and a half after college, I commuted five days a week between Lancaster and Lititz, eight miles away, where I taught in the high school. This line was graced by the last cars the company ever bought, big squat beasts with interurban pretensions, plush seats instead of the familiar old rattan, and the deep-toned, imperious whistles already mentioned. There were three regular crewmen on the run, who rotated from week to week as motorman and conductor by day and combination motorman-conductor by night. The senior man was John Smith (his real name), a portly, white-haired gentleman with dignity written all over him. John was known to everybody in Lititz, and his hourly trip down the town's main street to the end of the tracks, and back again, can only be described as a royal progress. On every block someone would wave to him, and John, at the controls, would nod gravely back, adding a measured, regal wave of the hand. His colleagues were, in comparison, vulgarians. Bink was short, stoop-shouldered, and if Dickens were writing this, I think he would have added dirty. Whereas John was cordial to his boarding passengers in a pleasantly formal way—"Good morning, gentlemen; how are you this fine morning?"— Bink was the uninhibited master of ceremonies, always good for a shady joke as he moved up and down the aisle collecting fares. The last member of the trio, Charlie, was banana-nosed and sardonic; he was the only one of the three to take a quick smoke at the Lititz end of the line.

The run, a quarter of it through city traffic, was barely achieved on a half-hour out, half-hour back schedule, and that meant that the line was famous, county-wide, for its speed and recklessness. When the car was in the company's right of way alongside the highway, the motorman had to keep the controller pushed to the very last notch. I still marvel at the fortitude of the rails in keeping us from leaping clear across the road into a field.

27

The big car roared over the rails across blind residential driveways from which at any moment an automobile might emerge. Once, as we were tearing down the Neffsville hill on the way to the city, a small delivery truck turned into a driveway ahead of us. Bink was at the controls that day, and though he had a right to expect that the truck was going to continue into the driveway at a safe distance from the tracks, he nevertheless applied the brakes and gave an extra, peremptory tug at the whistle cord. Instead of proceeding, the delivery man stopped cold on the tracks, as if he had entered the driveway simply to turn around. Bink danced up and down, yelling "Get that out of there!", and in desperation he reversed the car's motor in hope of aiding the brakes. For a long moment, as all of us sat with heartbeat and breath suspended, the car bore down on the truck. Then, just as a wreck seemed inevitable, the truck backed off and we flew past in a shower of dust and gravel, only inches from its fender. John, the conductor that day, who had been taking a rest on one of the back seats, removed his cap and silently fanned his brow with it. "Son of a bitch," Bink feelingly remarked to us as we disembarked, ashen-faced, at the Square.

These were the ingredients of a ride on the Lititz line, reckless speed, narrow escapes, and hospitality. Bink, John, and Charlie were more than crew members: they were hosts as well. If there were young lovers aboard on the night's last inbound run, whoever was motorman that night would turn off the lights. One day in the autumn, John, on his day off, boarded the car in a resplendent hunting outfit topped off by a jaunty Alpine hat complete with feather. Gun over his shoulder, he got off along the private right of way that wound through a patch of woods on Kissel Hill, just south of Lititz, followed by the jocose good wishes of the regulars. The next day, back in uniform, he reported a good day's hunting and favored us with explicit instructions on how to take the gamy taste out of pheasants. This I know happened, because I was there. But I cannot vouch for the truth of the other story about the line in hunting season, though it was a deathless legend among the passengers. According to the story, the crew once came to work armed with shotguns, and as the car slowly proceeded through those woods, the motorman would open the door and let the conductor try for a pheasant or a rabbit. On the return trip, the controls and the gun would change hands. If this didn't happen, there is no reason to believe that it couldn't have.

At midnight on Monday, 21 February 1938 (I made a note of it at the time), the Lititz trolley made its last trip, to be replaced in the morning by an upstart blue bus. All Lititz, I was told, turned out for the occasion. The lighted sign that usually read LITITZ was turned to FUNERAL. (Trolleys actually had been chartered to funeral parties in times past, a black flag, flying in the bracket usually reserved for a white flag, affirming, as a car swept by waiting passengers, that a "tripper"— second car—was following.) The passengers ate ice cream and pocketed small pieces of equipment for souvenirs; townspeople put torpedoes on the tracks. I am glad I was not there, because to me it was an occasion for sadness, not mindless rejoicing.

Growing up in any city necessarily means bottling in memory a rich Proustian mixture of sounds and odors that help define the sense of place one retains. The sounds: If the wind was from the east, West End dwellers could hear the chiming of the courthouse clock as well as the bell atop the nearest of the city's five firehouses. In the antiquated method of sounding the alarm that fell into disuse in the early 1920s, a street box was pulled at a certain location, and the electric impulses set the bell to ringing in a certain sequence; one then counted the strokes, and went to the front page of the telephone book which contained the code and found out where the fire was: one-two-three (pause) one-two-three-four meant, perhaps, the corner of Prince and Farnum. The fire engines themselves had bells with clappers and hand-cranked sirens. The emergency ambulances operated by the two hospitals, the General and St. Joseph's (there were no public-agency medic squads then), gave off a sustained gong sound like the continuous alarm in a modern building or the class-change signal in a school—*rrrrrrrring*—the duty intern and a white-capped nurse sitting in full view in the back as they sped toward a road accident.

At 9 p.m. the siren at the Armstrong linoleum plant, primarily used as an internal fire alarm, blew curfew, which meant that all juveniles were to be off the streets, an obedience, spelled out in a long-forgotten ordinance,

30

that was never enforced. More memorable was another sound, a kind of Sabbatarian curfew, that was provided by a church bell somewhere within hearing distance of my home. Its tolling about 7 p.m. on Sundays, calling people to the evening service, had a peculiarly melancholy timbre that I have never forgotten. I hear it every time I read Dickens's description, near the opening of *Little Dorrit*, of an interminable rainy Sunday, devoid of amusement and even of hope, in Victorian London.

A variety of sources contributed to one's Proustian collage of odorous associations. Under the right conditions, the (to me) not unpleasant smell of linseed oil spread over neighborhoods as much as a mile distant from Armstrong's. It was the only Lancastrian odor that was as pervasive on occasion as the perpetual aroma of cocoa for which the town of Hershey, some twenty-five miles to the northwest, was famous or notorious, depending on one's taste in airborne flavors. Other odors were more localized. The warehouses where leaf tobacco was stored sent out a characteristic sweetish redolence to passersby; Eshelman's feed and grain warehouse downtown, almost opposite the old depot, had a fragrance I identified as that of malt, though it may actually have come from some other grain. Passing Gunzenhauser's bakery at North Prince and Clay, one inhaled the delightful yeasty aroma of bread warm from the oven, and some blocks down the street there was the little Moseman store where peanuts were roasted and ground to be converted into peanut butter.

Indoors, there was the dry, mixed fragrance of spices

and freshly ground coffee that was the distinctive atmosphere of the self-serve grocery—many years before the advent of supermarkets—in the basement of Garvin's department store. Ordinary groceries on the ground level, like Seldomridge's downtown, didn't have as pronounced or individualized an odor as Garvin's did; I suppose that was because Garvin's had less ventilation. Passing a certain first-floor counter in one of the department stores, one had brief amalgamated whiffs of powders and perfumes, and flower shops like Barr's, whose orders I helped deliver during the rushes at Easter and Mother's Day, were a melange of sweet natural fragrances, somewhat overpowering until you got used to them. Better it, any day, than the strong odor of hot dogs and onions (what else besides?) that perpetually thickened the air at McCrory's and perhaps other variety stores that had quick-lunch counters, and the pungency of the gas works one passed on the Rocky Springs streetcar.

Memories of times and places are often moments of retinal persistence, casual, fleeting images seen long ago and thought nothing of at the time, but remaining fixed in the inner eye across the years. So it is with the synthesized scenes by which my imagination recollects Lancaster seasons, particularly summer and winter. Until recently, a remembered Lancaster in summer meant an unlocalized scene dominated by a big dark red brick building, a warehouse or factory on an unidentified street, with the sun high in the sky and the temperature in the sweltering nineties; nobody is in sight, but perhaps I am myself walking along the sidewalk and sweating.

But this momentary snapshot dissolves into another one. I haven't the slightest notion why I envision a Lancaster summer evening in terms of the intersection of First and Ruby Streets—the mere existence, at the corner, of a small neighborhood café that served good crabcakes with the beer advertised by the neon sign in the window has no bearing on my choice. First and Ruby was in a lower middle-class neighborhood, some blocks from my home. It had no association whatsoever with any incident in my life. Yet there it is after dark, dominated by an arc light suspended from the arm of a utility pole, and on it I build a scenario. The day has been hot and humid—the two ordinarily went together in southeastern Pennsylvania—and the evening is scarcely less so. The neighborhood kids are gathered at the corner, under the arc light whose stammering and stuttering produces a kind of audible blink. Moths flit and flutter about its globe, and a bat or two swoops toward it from the shadows. There is the periodic dry rasp of tree toads (or are they locusts?). What the kids are talking about in their childish or postpubertal voices, I don't know; they are simply passing the time—it's too hot to be indoors. Adults are sitting on their front porches or steps, fanning themselves. (Houses built with Lancastrian solidity retained a certain amount of coolness during the day, but not enough to tempt one to remain indoors after dusk, and the uninsulated roofs meant that the sleeping rooms and attics were like ovens.) Through the open windows of several houses near the corner pours the cacophony of radios tuned to different stations: a "news commentator"—the term was a novelty then—on one, a popular comedy show on another, a dance orchestra on a third. (If this scene were set a little earlier, at 7 p.m., all radios would have been tuned to one show, "Amos 'n' Andy," which dominated the airwaves at that hour and caused people to change their habitual routines so it wouldn't be missed.)

The merged radio programs are periodically interrupted by fits of scratchy static from some disturbance in the atmosphere that may be building up to a thunderstorm. Or perhaps there already is at intervals the silent momentary flush of heat lightning on the horizon. As the evening wears on and street-corner bickering sets in, the kids' voices become more shrill, the radios continue to cough. Perhaps the lightning to the south, though still silent, grows more vivid, and people will say "They're getting it in Quarryville," or if it is in the opposite direction they will say "It must be raining in Manheim." And then the lightning in the west, the direction from which most thunderstorms come, grows brighter, and there are claps of thunder, and the leading edge of the storm arrives, with a strong wind that stirs up the dust and sends the kids scattering to their homes and a blinding downpour of rain accompanied by nearby snaps of lightning and crashing thunder. People run inside to close their windows. Soon the gutters are gushing. Half an hour later, the storm has passed into eastern Lancaster County and, seen from First and Ruby, it has faded back into heat lightning. The trees drip, the arc light stutters on; the temperature has dropped ten degrees, and people open their windows again and come out to sit again on their porches to gratefully breathe in the cleansed air before going to bed.

But suppose, now, it's winter in Lancaster. The retentive imagination is focused not on a single small locale but on a temporal panorama, beginning at night on a perfectly unremarkable street in the Sixth Ward, where the windows of the small row houses that have no porches but only concrete stoops are lighted with little electric candelabras, and inside, seen through the windows, the winking lights and tinsel of Christmas trees. A day or two earlier there has been a snowfall. The snow on the humped brick sidewalk has melted during the day, but now the slush has refrozen into ice, and in the darkness, illumined only by a nearby street lamp, you must pick your way cautiously to avoid a fall.

It is, for choice, Christmas Eve, and Lancaster externally is in the state of suspended animation into which it fell at precisely six o'clock. This is the hour when the stores closed and the month-long shopping season irrevocably ended. I, for one, am grateful, because since Thanksgiving I have been in the midst of the crescendoing bustle at Watt and Shand's department store, the Lancastrian equivalent of Philadelphia's Wanamaker's, either on a delivery truck or, more recently, a salesperson in the boys' clothing department, and I have had it with Christmas and all its manifestations. The last few days, the clock over the store elevators, hopefully

35

watched from the selling floor, seemed to have virtually
stopped between four-thirty and six, so invisible was the
hands' progress.

The downtown streets have a plethora of seasonal
decorations: the lamp posts are hung with lighted
wreaths, and festoons of green roping and strings of
bulbs have been draped over the facades of the larger
stores, accompanied by painted plywood cutouts of
Santa Claus and his reindeer, angelic-faced, candle- or
lantern-bearing child carolers, or other appropriate
subjects. Salvation Army "lassies" (the word a carryover
from the World War, when they were so named by the
soldiers to whom they served coffee and doughnuts),
red-cheeked and runny of nose under their black sugar-
scoop bonnets, the men in their black uniforms with red
bands on their visored caps saying SALVATION ARMY
in gold, each standing on a little wooden platform to
reduce the effect of the damp, cold sidewalks and yet all
stamping their feet even if they are shod in galoshes or
rubbers, ceaselessly tinkled their little bells. Crowds of
shoppers moved from store to store, Watt and Shand's
and Hager's upmarket, Penney's and Garvin's middle-
market; if you wanted to give someone jewelry or a clock,
you got a price at Zook's or Weber's (decidedly upmarket) and, if your money was running low, you bought a
cheaper equivalent down the street at Kranich's, where
you could get terms.

The air, in fact, was heavy and hectic with Christmas.
But finally, six o'clock has come. The downtown streets
are deserted, though their glittering show windows are

36

still lighted and the exterior decorations glow bravely on—irrelevantly, because nobody is around to have his holiday spirit reinforced by them. In the residential sections, only the seasonal carriers of mail are still abroad with their last deliveries: the khaki-painted National Guard trucks that have been called into service to supplement the post office's olive-green parcel post trucks, and the college students who have left their classes early to make spending money by trudging alongside the regular postmen, their leather pouches slung professionally over their shoulders. With these belated exceptions, Lancaster has reached its annual condition of utter exhaustion.

There will be midnight masses at the Catholic churches and in the chapel of St. Joseph's Hospital, with its attendance of patients in wheelchairs and white-habited sisters, but these will be discontinued as Lancaster people, whether Catholics or not, begin to make a yearly custom of dropping in after alcoholic parties. On the Hamilton Watch Company grounds on the western edge of town (about these, more later), all the big old evergreens, some twenty or thirty all told, are draped with strings of red and green lights. Midway on the Columbia Avenue frontage there is an illuminated creche scene, painted by a local artist. At stated hours, five o'clock when the workers are going home and again at eight o'clock, loudspeakers on the clock towers at both ends of the long building pour forth a recorded program of Christmas songs played on off-pitch chimes, to unbearably lugubrious effect. Having suffered the tinny tintinnabulation of those bells, season after season, for most of my young life—our home was just across the street—I have an ineradicable prejudice against Christmas carols. But the whole display was a notable ritual event in the Lancaster winter, and on Christmas night and New Year's Eve long lines of cars filled with sightseers crept along Columbia Avenue and up our street.

A Lancaster Christmas did have its unambiguous delights for children. At least one big hardware store, Sprecher and Gantz, and the department stores cleared much space in their year-round toy departments to devote it to elaborate electric train layouts, with lots of tracks, sidings, switches, papier mâché mountains, tunnels, mirrored lakes and rivers, towns with street lighting and operative crossing gates. But even these Lilliputian spectacles, so authentic in detail if not in overall, somewhat chaotic, impression, were outdone by the Christmas yards, as they were called, at the city firehouses. There, the firemen moved their apparatus elsewhere, leaving behind, however, one shining horse-drawn steam pumper, relic of a bygone day: I wonder into what museum it eventually was trundled. If the train displays in the stores could be measured in to-scale miniature acres, those in the firehouses seemed to cover square miles. And all were free to see.

More likely than not, at this time of year, there would be snow on the ground, deposited by one of those storms that swept up the seaboard and then turned inland. *Much* snow; in good seasons, as much as a foot or eighteen inches at a time. There was much relish in being indoors during a blizzard, the soft snow swirling in dense clouds, drifts mounting, the tires of the creeping cars making soft crunching sounds in the snow. The most seasonal of non-carolian sounds was the scrape of shovels on the sidewalks after the storm abated. The piles of snow, growing dirtier by the day along the streets but keeping their pristine whiteness elsewhere, might remain for weeks. If the streets were well packed to make a slippery surface, an occasional sleigh, brought out from somebody's outlying barn or loft, might drive by with jingling bells on the horse's harness, as marked a relic of a former day as the city's few electric broughams, severely square and as upright as the ladies wearing Queen Mary toques who steered them with a tiller, would soon become.

There was good sledding, in cold sunshine or under arc lights, on some streets in the Eighth Ward (Cabbage Hill) and at Buchanan Park. There was also good ice skating at two places west of town. One was Herr's pond, adjacent to a building where artificial ice was made throughout the year, to be transported downtown in hundred-pound cakes by slow-moving electric trucks. Just beyond it, at the Maple Grove amusement park, now closed for the winter, was the flooded floor of a disused quarry, which had the advantage of protection from the biting January wind.

Christmas was the crowning holiday of the year. But there were others, notably the Fourth of July, which was ushered in, practically at dawn, by the crackles, pops, and bangs of fireworks, not only nearby but heard from

a distance before there was much traffic noise. These
explosions continued without remission throughout the
day, with sparkling color added after nightfall. Until
fireworks were made illegal, except for organized displays, the newspapers the next day ran columns listing
all the children and adults who had been treated for
burns or puncture wounds at the hospital emergency
rooms. In our neighborhood, the big event of the day
was Uncle Billy Lebzelter's party. Uncle Billy was Lancaster's version of a middle-aged *rentier*, having no
visible occupation but seemingly well fixed with an income from a tire dealership downtown. He had a home
with a spacious yard across from Hamilton Watch, and
there, every Fourth of July, he played host in his red,
white, and blue shirt, never worn except on this day, to
an enthusiastic crowd of kids. The feature entertainer
was a magician-ventriloquist named Ned Frailey, whose
Adam's apple moved up and down when he conversed
with the dummy he held on his lap, à la Edgar Bergen
and Charlie McCarthy. I seem to recall that once or
twice he set up a Punch and Judy show instead. After
the performance there was plenty of ice cream, Cracker
Jack, and other foods and favors, but eventually too
many kids and free-loading adults turned up from other
neighborhoods, and Uncle Billy reluctantly had to give
up his parties.

This was all Time Present: what about Time Past?
Overlaid on the image of modern Lancaster I acquired,
detail by detail, as I walked, biked, and rode delivery

trucks, and lending it temporal depth, was the image that spoke of the past. It was supplied to me, virtually as soon as I was able to read, by whatever examples of Chamber of Commerce promotional literature came my way, confirmed and amplified by the descriptions I hunted out in reference works. I must have had an innate predisposition to history, which, come to think of it, may have had something to do with my own ancestry. Colonel Matthias Slough, a Revolution-era forebear of my mother, was landlord of the White Swan Inn, Lancaster's premier hostelry, on the site on the Square that was later occupied by Watt and Shand's store. His, and the inn's, proudest moment came when they entertained— "royally" would doubtless be an inappropriate word to use in this context—the leaders of the Continental Congress during their overnight stay in September 1777. The precious Declaration of Independence was kept in a wagon, under guard, in the courtyard. (It is, I suppose, neither here nor there that I have tavern-keeping blood from both sides of my family. My paternal grandmother, Mary Graeff, was a daughter of the man who ran an old inn (1784) at Graeff's Landing, where the bridge south of Lancaster crossed the Conestoga.)

In any event, I lapped up all the information about Lancaster's past that came my way, and venerated it as precious, unquestionable truth. It is fair to say that I was brainwashed from an early age. Two-hundred-year-old Lancaster, it appeared, had a history to be proud of.

Most settled communities in America had, by that

41

date, some kind of past they sought to use; few were so
new as to lack some fodder for local boosterism. Like
many counties in the eastern states, Lancaster had two
or three distinct strata of place names that implied a
longish history, from those applied by the eighteenth-
century settlers to several, such as Oregon and Lincoln,
that memorialized events of less than a hundred years
ago. There was also, as I have noted, the specifically
colonial flavor of the city's street names. But such an
array of signpost names, while epitomizing a good deal
of history if anyone troubled to track down the origin of
each, was not unique to Lancaster. These commonplace
symbols were not in themselves the sort of data that
could be made into a packagable commodity with which
to advertise the city and county. What was needed was
recognizable names and dates, relating to a past that
long since had become the standard content of school-
books and the common fund of patriotic sentiment—
matters of national interest, in short. Lancaster, fortunately, was so old that it could boast not only of a
thriving present but an equally thriving, and what is
more, highly creditable past: it had been in business
before the nation was born.

I cannot help thinking that Lancaster's position within
Philadelphia's zone of influence had much to do with the
picture it cultivated of itself, both for its own satisfaction
and the favorable regard of others. Philadelphia, too,
was a modern city, the third largest in the United States
in the 1920–40 period, many times the size of Lancaster;
but it also had roots that struck deep in the eighteenth-

century soil. What with its early founding by William Penn and his peace-loving Quaker friends, the Horatio Alger-type saga of Benjamin Franklin, and its role as the site of redcoated officers' revelry while Washington's frostbitten and starving army huddled around the campfires at Valley Forge, Philadelphia could well claim to be the most "historic" city in the United States, even though Boston was a strong competitor. Lancaster's implicit claim was that it was a miniature Philadelphia, with one foot in the Harding-Coolidge-Hoover era, which at that time was nothing to be ashamed of, and the other firmly planted on patriotic earth.

And so Lancastrians and the world in general were reminded, time and time again, that Lancaster had been the capital of the rebellious colonies for one memorable day in 1777; that its industries had armed Washington's army and, a little later, outfitted wagon trains heading for the broad unsettled lands beyond the Alleghenies; that from 1760 to the early nineteenth century it had been the new nation's largest inland city; that Robert Fulton, inventor of the steamboat, was a native son; that the artist Benjamin West, the future president of Britain's prestigious Royal Academy, had Lancaster associations; that one of the signers of the Declaration of Independence came from there.

To bridge the present with the honorable, if not actually heroic, past, local boosters never tired of pointing out that Demuth's tobacco shop was the oldest such business in the country that remained in the hands of the family that had founded it, in Revolutionary days, and that Steinman's hardware store and Hager's department store were ditto in their respective lines. Franklin and Marshall College had been founded in 1787, and it was now very much of a presence up near the twin water towers. Lancaster's marketable glory therefore was not limited to past events, but further distinguished by the continuity of its institutions.

As for the century that intervened between, say, the departure of the first pioneers' wagon trains and F.W. Woolworth's successful venture in cut-rate retailing, Lancaster could point out that James Buchanan, a member of the local bar, had resided before and after his presidency in a modest mansion, Wheatland, on the Marietta Pike just outside the city. A leading politician of the Reconstruction era, the controversial Thaddeus Stevens, whose name, like Buchanan's, was preserved in a number of Lancaster's business and institutional titles, was buried in a cemetery behind the Boys' High School. But that was just about it.

To a youth so firmly persuaded of his city's place in history, there was disappointingly little to see. It appeared that the people who shaped nineteenth-century Lancaster had no great interest in preserving the past in physical form. Nearly all the housing within the city limits, and most of it in the outlying towns, dated from the later half of the nineteenth century or the first decade of the twentieth. A small number of row houses on North Duke and East Orange Streets were said to date from colonial times, but they bore no plaques and were not singled out in any promotional literature. Trinity Lutheran Church was the only public building that preserved the graceful eighteenth-century style. It was said to have been designed by Sir Christopher Wren, but, the dates not fitting (Wren died in 1723), the best that could be said of it as a historical monument was that it was inspired by some of Wren's churches in the City of London with their chaste white interiors and three-sided balconies.

I did have a momentary glimpse of the distant past—it may, indeed, have predated even the Buchanan Park airplane—when I saw on Columbia Avenue (the westward extension of West King Street), pulled by teams of straining horses, the blue cradle-shaped chassis of a Conestoga wagon, bereft of the prairie schooner's cylindrical canvas hood. It was hauling a load of stone from the Maple Grove quarry to some destination in town. I never learned what its history was, or what happened to it; I hope it is now preserved, with the steam fire engine, in some museum. Otherwise, if you didn't count the weathered tombstones in the enclosed cemetery of St. James's Episcopal Church at Duke and Orange, or those at a scattering of old churches in the county, such as Donegal Presbyterian near the Dauphin County line, the past was signally lacking in tangibility.

One homely detail, doubtless noticed by no one else, epitomized to me the Lancaster of somewhat more recent vintage, the turn-of-the-century years when my father's family had a prosperous carriage-building business. This was the antiquated style of business names surviving in fading paint on the walls or above the doors of old

45

buildings: the abbreviations JNO. (for John), GEO., JAS., BENJ., EDW., & BRO., the name of the firm always concluding with a decided, no-nonsense period, the rationale for which I have yet to discover. Because these designations were no longer current, yet could be seen in hundreds of places, they were a distinctive, and to me flavorful, reminder of past customs.

The general lack of physical vestiges, however, never dampened Lancaster's enthusiasm for backward-looking, nor mine. I had the far richer history of Philadelphia to assist my imaginative re-creation of eighteenth-century Lancaster. At one point, I discovered Paul Leicester Ford's novel of life in wartime Philadelphia, *Janice Meredith*, and I could hardly wait until the film based on it came to town. Twice—for the sesquicentennial of the Declaration of Independence in 1926 and for the county's bicentennial in 1929—the community mustered all its resources to put on elaborate night-time pageants on the college's football field. Heavy with patriotic allegory, explained by elocutionary voices from loudspeakers, and replete with dramatizations of landmark events—I was one of the kids who were assigned to run alongside General Lafayette's coach as he visited Lancaster during his triumphant return to the States in 1825—these *son et lumière* productions did much to bolster Lancaster's confidence that it had a great story to tell.

The local historical tradition had a minor backup that reached much further into history, having no American connections at all. The names Lancaster and York of course recalled the fifteenth-century English Wars of the Roses, and thus it was inevitable that Lancaster came to call itself the Red Rose City, along with being the Garden Spot of America, the Home of the Hamilton Watch, etc., etc. Sometime in the 1930s, some voluntary organization, probably a garden club, planted red rose bushes along the western reach of the Lincoln Highway, to complement the white ones a similar group from York planted on its side of the Susquehanna. I don't think they lasted long. But one other tangible reminder of the twilight of feudalism was indestructible: the Lancaster County jail on East King Street, which was said to have been modeled after the castle in Lancaster, England. The English and American Lancasters were, in fact, sister cities, and on at least one occasion ceremonially exchanged mayors.

From this small catalog of Lancastrian reminders of the past I have omitted the one physical presence that compensated for all the deficiencies. On the downtown streets on market days and in the markets themselves, and every day along the country roads and in the little villages with hitching posts, the eighteenth century still lived. It was almost as if, in the Philadelphia of the 1920s, a noticeable number of men, women, and children, dressed as Quakers would have been in William Penn's day, had mingled with the daytime crowds on Market Street or Broad Street. Lancaster, however, had it all over Philadelphia in point of authenticity, because the "plain people" on King or Queen Street were no mere dressed-up walk-ons; they were part of no stunt.

47

In custom as well as costume, they were a remarkably unassimilated throwback to a time separated from the present by two hundred years. They were, in a sense, Lancaster's oldest inhabitants. They belonged.

THE PEOPLE

We were some 60,000 men, women, and children. (Perhaps I should exclude myself, because we lived a hundred feet or so beyond the city limits.) Lancaster's population, like its economy and its social climate, was stable; it remained at that figure for two decades. But the census figures for the city did not reflect the gradual spillover into the adjoining townships. Nobody thought of lumping the inside and peripheral populations together and calling the result "metro." A city's population was what the United States Census Bureau said it was, no more, no less.

As any visitor to Lancaster immediately noticed, the German element predominated. The business signs and the telephone directory abounded in family names of a sort found nowhere else in such profusion. Some took the form of tight-lipped monosyllables that made up in concision what they lacked in euphony: Herr, Funk, Good, Shenk, Getz, Hess, Gantz, Shirk, Shimp, Shoop, Erb, Kling, Fry, Glick, Stump, Kuntz, Kutz (the "u" in the latter three was pronounced as in "took"). But polysyllabic names were just as numerous, and some were of such extravagance as to suggest—or is this merely my whimsy?—the curlicues of northern Baroque architecture: Gochenaur, Diffenderffer, Sensenig, Finnefrock, Schneebeli (often converted into Snavely), Druckenbrod, Eichelberger, Sullenberger, Dunkelberger, Gladfelter, Espenshade, Gingrich (rhymed with Minnick), Kreider, Brackbill, Brubaker, Shertzer, Mellinger, Metzger, Spangler, Garber, Kunkle, Witmer, Smeltzer . . . and Hipple, Gibble, and Pickle. These particular names are found in quantity in few American localities beyond Lancaster. Other mixes, equally "Dutch," are found in the counties to the northeast, around Reading, Bethlehem, Kutztown, and Allentown.

By bringing from the Rhineland and Switzerland their farming expertise along with their mastery of other trades, bearers of such names had made Lancaster what its promoters proudly announced it was, the richest agricultural county in the United States. Living in farmhouses of native gray fieldstone to which additions had often been made as families grew and new generations succeeded the old on the land, they tilled one- or two-hundred-acre farms, producing grain crops, broadleaved tobacco for cigars, vegetables, and fruits. Some spreads were, wholly or in part, stock or dairy farms, sending fattened cattle to distant markets by way of the whitewashed sheds and pens ("the largest stockyards east of Chicago") that lined the railroad at the northern edge of the city, and milk, picked up by trucks at roadside platforms, to Philadelphia and the chocolate factories in Lancaster, Hershey, Mount Joy, and Lititz. The absolute neatness of the fields and buildings was as much admired as the management of the land. Lancaster County farmers were rotating and diversifying their crops long before the New Deal rural conservation agencies in the mid-1930s showed others how to do it.

Actually (it is a point often obscured when people talk and write about the Pennsylvania Dutch) the German population had two distinct components. One, decidedly the more numerous, comprised two mainstream—in fact the oldest—Protestant denominations, Lutheran and Reformed (Calvinist). Their forebears had brought their affiliations intact from Europe, and in their new home they had no peculiarities that set them apart from their English-speaking neighbors except their language and family names. They retained the names, but their use of the Pennsylvania Dutch dialect, except occasionally as a second language, had faded to the point of extinction by the end of the nineteenth century. And, most important, they had no scruples about keeping up with the times. They represented the cutting edge of modernity, such as it was, in the Lancaster setting. These were the people whom their "plain" neighbors called, before the word acquired a very different meaning, "gay." That is, they saw no harm in indulging in such harmless vanities of the world as personal ornamentation. They were God-fearing enough, but they did not conceive of God's wrath descending on them for any reason having to do with the way they dressed.

In the popular mind, however, "Pennsylvania Dutch" was synonymous with the other component of the Lancaster population, those who were set apart by the clothing they wore, essentially unaltered since, as members of pietistic sects for whom their homeland held no peace, they came to seek the freer air of the New World. Generically but inaccurately known simply as "the Amish" (pronounced "ommish"), they consisted not only of the Amish but Mennonites as well, the older sect from whom the Amish had broken off because of doctrinal differences. A third sect, resembling the Amish rather than the Mennonites in dress, were the Dunkards, or Brethren. In the aggregate, they set their visible and cultural seal on the Lancaster landscape.

The Amish, settled for the most part in the eastern half of the county, were the most scruple-bound people who ever settled in America in any significant numbers, even more so than the New England Puritans, from whom they differed, however, in their refusal to assimilate into the general population. They kept a rigorous distance from modern inventions and conveniences: no automobiles (though they could ride in other people's if not for pleasure), no indoor plumbing, no electricity, no telephones (but they could use pay phones along the road). They used farm machinery, so long as it was not self-propelled; horse- or mule-drawn reapers were sanctioned, tractors were not. In addition to farming, they followed farm-related trades, so that their dependence on others outside the faith was kept to a minimum. There were skilled Amish carpenters, masons, blacksmiths, and wheelwrights. They not only grew their own food but built their own barns as well as the black and gray box-like buggies, curtained against the weather, in which they traversed the country roads. Musical instruments were taboo on scriptural grounds, and radios by extension of the same principle.

The Amish withdrew their children from school at the earliest moment the law allowed, a practice that was to bring them into protracted conflict with state law after the Second World War, when the one-room schoolhouses whose pupils were mostly if not all Amish were giving way to consolidated ones. In addition to the danger of being corrupted by their classmates' "modern" ways, the children, they feared, might be overeducated for their destined way of life, which was to till the land as their ancestors had done. The Amish were also pacifists, and although they were always good taxpaying citizens, except when this legal obligation conflicted with their religion, they voted only for local offices and occupied them only when there was no alternative. They refused to accept the subsidies the New Deal offered them.

The Amish spoke English only as a second language. They were a self-contained society, never proselytizing, admitting no newcomers, even by marriage, and simply writing off the rare independent-minded men and women among them who were seduced by the outside world as represented by the manners and morals of, say, Lancaster city. They were inbred to the extent that their mailboxes along the R.F.D. routes bore no more than a dozen family names: Zook, Miller, Stoltzfus, Lapp,

King, Smoker, Martin, Hostetler, Gish, Mast, Yoder, Beiler. The men's given names were drawn exclusively from the Old Testament, with stress on the prophets and patriarchs: Benjamin, Noah, Amos, Levi, Isaac, Jacob, Aaron, Eli, Moses, Abraham. The women's names were equally biblical: Naomi, Sarah, Esther, Amanda, Leah, Reba. It is not surprising that in recent years the Amish have proved to be prime material for sociological and genetic research centering on closed societies.

They had no mirrors in their houses and were forbidden to have their pictures taken, a prohibition that led to touchy situations when outside photographers, journalists as well as sightseers, began to discover how "quaint" the Amish were. Their eschewal of personal vanity was most evident in the clothes they wore. Quintessential utility and modesty, not fashion or the urge for personal expression through individuality, marked every inch of their garb. Most was homemade and devoid of buttons, which were vain; pins and hooks and eyes— and latterly zippers!—were the only acceptable fasteners, because they were invisible. Men's suits were black and utterly without ornament. Their hats were black (straw in the summer) and flat-crowned and -brimmed. They were clean-shaven until they married, after which they all wore beards but no moustaches. Like the Puritan Roundheads in seventeenth-century England, they wore their hair lanky and long, in a fashion suggesting the large bowl that was actually used for kitchen haircuts.

Women's clothing was made to a pattern that had been standard in the northern Europe their ancestors had left behind. It can be seen to some extent in seventeenth-century Dutch and Flemish paintings, especially of peasant life though some of the details found their way into the bourgeois towns of the time. The ankle-length dresses were cut close to the neck, with an extra triangular piece coming to a point in front and back. Although the cloth was never figured, it might be colored, with the result that Amishmen in their unrelieved black (except for their shirts) had wives dressed in bright blue, purple, green, or russet. The women wore large black bonnets with tie strings under the chin and ruffles in the back, and under the bonnets, worn indoors as well as outdoors, "prayer caps" or "prayer coverings," bonnet shaped but made of white voile, their tie strings usually hanging loose beneath the chin.

Children's clothing, also homemade, turned them into accurate miniature replicas of their parents: the same cut of trousers and coats for the boys (and the same haircuts), the same vividly colored but strictly unadorned dresses for the girls, and, after a certain age, prayer caps as well.

This is the way the Amish looked when one saw them driving their single-horse buggies along the roads east of Lancaster or buying supplies at general stores with hitching racks outside in such towns as Ephrata, New Holland, and Blue Ball. Twice a week, some of them sold their produce at one or another of the Lancaster markets; less often, they came to town to visit a family member in one of the hospitals, see a specialist physician, or transact business that could not be taken care of in the county, such as filing a deed in the county courthouse. In earlier years, they drove their buggies or market wagons into town; by the 1920s, when city traffic presented too much of a problem, they either came by trolley or got a ride with a more worldly neighbor who had a car.

Peasants they may have been in respect to their deep rooting in the soil and their no-frills way of life, but unlike their European counterparts in a former age they were independent. As their own landlords, producers of commodities that were theirs alone, to sell as they wished, they were beholden to no one. And they took care of their own when, for one reason or another, they needed help. A barn burned, and the Amish for miles around came to raise a new one in a single day, the women providing the bounteous meals and everybody treating the occasion as a festive holiday sanctified by its altruistic purpose. There was no such word as "welfare" in the Pennsylvania Dutch vocabulary.

There may have been poor Amishmen, but how could you tell? They all dressed alike, and none, including the wives, wore any such incidental indications of wealth as jewelry. The men spent nothing on themselves except for necessities, but they were shrewd businessmen, they got good prices for their crops and stock, and the worth of their land steadily increased. And, as a matter of fact, more than a few Amishmen were reputed to be well to do by any contemporary measure of wealth. A joke bandied about Lancaster had it that an Amishman and his wife came to a bank to close the purchase of an adjoining farm for one of their sons. The man carefully counted out ninety thousand dollars in bills from his purse, but this was ten thousand short of the farm's agreed-upon price. "Ach, Pop," said his wife, "you brought the wrong purse."

There were two sub-genera of Amish, the "house" Amish who had no churches but held services in rotation at their respective homes, where, on a Sunday, as many as thirty or forty buggies might be parked, and the "meeting house" Amish. Services were presided over by bishops, but there were no full-time clergy: every Amish preacher was a farmer or a craftsman as well. Their meeting houses were as austere as their clothing. Like the other "plain" denominations, they had strict rules of conduct. Liquor was not tolerated, and tobacco barely, despite the money they made from the crop. The greatest indulgence an Amishman allowed himself on a visit to Lancaster was a cheap cigar. On such an excursion, he might also treat his wife and wide-eyed children to ice cream sodas at a confectionery. But their deviation from rigorous self-denial went no further than this. Or so it struck an outsider. Within their community they had their own entertainments, not only the periodic barn-raisings but quilting bees and simple visiting around; after all, in so closed a society everybody knew everybody else and, in view of their intermarriage, everybody was related to everybody else. Teenagers, in addition to courting in buggies whose horse knew the way even if the reins were slack, had their wilder moments. When the Pennsylvania Turnpike was under construction through northern Lancaster County they were said to have raced their buggies on the concrete roadway before it was open for traffic. Their elders might have told them that that was no way to treat their horses' feet.

Among themselves, the Amish spoke their own language, a dialect *of* a German dialect. Their English was flavored with German idioms and constructions, some of which found their way into the vocabularies of their non-plain neighbors, including urban Lancastrians. Many allegedly Pennsylvania Dutch expressions were, even then, being fabricated for the gullible outsider, but I can vouch for the authenticity of such phrases as "redding up" (putting a cluttered room or desk top in order: curiously, this is also a Scotticism), "what does the weather want?" (what does the weather report predict?), "it looks like it might give rain," "the tooth doesn't ouch any longer," "stop rutching" (squirming). Sometimes the mingling of English and German had odd results. I once overheard a woman in Ephrata asking her husband where their buggy was ge-parkt.

The Amish, then, were a self-contained social phenomenon, a pocket of the Old World of two centuries ago through which the Pennsy's main line cut without disturbing them in the least. There was no significant social or cultural association between the plain people and their neighbors. Seldom did any of the latter attend an Amish service or have a meal in an Amish farmhouse. As a matter of fact, plenty of Lancaster people, myself included, never set foot in *any* barnyard or farmhouse, so citified were we.

The people in Lancaster and the surrounding towns to the east and north who knew the Amish best were the bankers, cattle dealers, wholesale buyers of farm produce including tobacco, dealers in feed and farm equipment, and whoever in addition frequented the auction sales which the horse-and-buggy drivers regularly attended, both as a social occasion and in quest of second-hand bargains for the home and barn. The country businessmen had great respect for the plain people, whose reputation for honest dealing was immaculate, and such stories as were told of them were totally without spite. Other contacts were more *ad hoc*: there were always a few Lancaster people who knew of an Amishman "down back of" Strasburg who was an expert cabinet-maker or an Amish woman somewhere on a road near Leola who made particularly good shoofly pies or scrapple, and they would drive their cars right to the shop or farm to avail themselves of such rare talent.

The Mennonites were also plain people, but they were less extreme in their dress and taboos. Although most were farmers, in the period of which I am writing an increasing number were leaving the land for the country towns and Lancaster itself, to become small businessmen, bookkeepers, skilled artisans and house builders, even automobile mechanics. (They drove cars, but when chrome trimmings came into fashion, they painted them black.) Since the Mennonites had nothing against secondary education, many boys and girls finished high school and if they were not needed at home the girls became store clerks or office help. A few even went to one or other of the colleges of their denomination, in Harrisonburg, Virginia, and Goshen, Indiana.

Mennonites had their own distinctive clothing. Men's suits, conservative but store-bought, were notable for the collar- and lapel-less style to be associated much later with Nehru and Mao Zedong. Neckties were not worn, and men's hats were a modified version of the Amish model. They could not, however, be tipped. Mr. Enos Weaver, a pleasant neighbor of ours, held his hands out before him when he met a woman on the sidewalk, to imply that they held a parcel which prevented him from raising his hat. Mennonite women's bonnets were not as large as Amish women's, and their dresses, though they might be an inch or two shorter, were cut along Amish lines. But whereas Amish women went in for bright colors, the Mennonites wore black or gray. As if in compensation for this sacrifice, they could make their dresses from cloth with tiny figures, a concession un-available to the Amish. Mennonite women too wore prayer coverings, but a telltale sign of creeping seculari-zation was the way young women were gradually allowing their caps to shrink in size. What originally had been an adornment in the shape of a sugar scoop diminished until, by the 1940s, on some heads it had become no bigger than a doll's handkerchief, a vestigial wisp of white material to denote a nominal affiliation with the church. Pinned into the hair of the most emancipated Mennonite girls, it might easily have been mistaken for a passing whim of feminine fashion.

Although Mennonite custom, like the Amish, forbade

dancing, bowling, movie-going and other secular recreation, no scruple prevented their having electricity and bathrooms in their homes, which might be comfortably, though never luxuriously, furnished. And although there was strong pressure to marry within the faith, a few Mennonites married outsiders, and some even left to join one of the non-plain denominations. This accounted for the presence in the homes of Lancaster city families, themselves Lutherans or Methodists, of an elderly grandmother or maiden aunt who retained her Mennonite dress and full-sized prayer cap—a sign that at some time or other a son or daughter had "crossed over."

The Mennonites in town and country worshipped in red-brick, slate-roofed oblong boxes that were sedulously devoid of decoration inside and out; they did not have steeples. In contrast, the mainstream denominations tended toward the heavy Henry Ward Beecher Ecclesiastic style, stone on the outside, stained glass, wooden pews, and carved ornamentation inside. In my admittedly limited, and possibly resistant, experience, they did nothing to lift the spirit. They were the essence of dully conventional late-nineteenth-century taste, undistinguishable from thousands of other churches in American cities.

Within the denominations there was a clear pecking order. The Episcopalians enjoyed the highest social standing; set apart from most of the other Protestant communions in that they were mostly of Anglo-Scots rather than German descent, they constituted a small elite. Their two parishes reflected the division prevalent in the Anglican Church itself: the older, St. James's, with its enclosed tree-shaded graveyard at the downtown corner of Duke and Orange, was high church, whereas St. John's, a few blocks away, was low. Next in rank, and again reflecting the non-German strain in the city, were the Presbyterians. Tied for third place, so far as I could observe, were four denominations: the Lutheran and Reformed, both predominantly German in derivation, and the Evangelical and Methodist, somewhat less so. The Baptists had no special social distinction. A little apart from these were the Moravians, another denomination with its roots in Central Europe—its American headquarters was in Bethlehem, Pennsylvania—and the town Mennonites. There was the usual movement between the churches, a Lutheran, for whatever reasons— perhaps marriage, perhaps convenience of location— becoming a Presbyterian. And to the upward mobile, socially ambitious families, the Episcopalian communion beckoned: to move to it from, say, the Reformed represented a definite step toward improving one's position in local society.

On the perilous outer edge of Protestantism, doctrinally speaking, were the Unitarians, who represented New England-derived liberal thought in a generally conservative city; it was no accident that the meeting room attached to their church in the West End was named Emerson Hall. Among their members could be counted most of the Lancastrians (not numerous in any case) who read the *Nation* and the *New Republic* every week, looked with favor on co-ops, had severe bouts of political con-

science when the presidential ballot offered a choice
between Franklin D. Roosevelt and Norman Thomas,
and would have been in the forefront of the civil rights
movement if one had existed.

Off to one side, and socially the most comprehensive,
were the five Roman Catholic churches, which made a
strong showing against the broad representation of Protestant faiths. The oldest, preserving memories of Lancaster's first (in two senses) Catholic families, was St.
Mary's, downtown. St. Joseph's served Cabbage Hill,
which was German with a sprinkling of Italians. (There
were few Irish families in town.) Only a purist outside
the rectory would say "St. Joseph's"; in popular speech,
including sports articles in the newspapers, it was always
the easygoing, to me over-familiar "St. Joe's." If "St.
Joe's" was acceptable, why not call St. Anthony's, out in
the East End, "St. Tony's" or, for that matter, speak of
St. Mary's as "St. Mame's"? But they didn't have the
strong basketball teams that St. Joe's did.

Black-habited nuns with their starched wimples were
not often seen on Lancaster streets, but when they were,
they were as noticeable as Amish families. Their daily
routine did not bring them very much into public view,
because they merely shuttled the short distances that
separated their convents, mysterious, reclusive buildings
that both invited and repelled the curiosity of passersby,
and the adjacent parochial schools where they taught or
St. Joseph's Hospital, where, in white habits, they
tended the sick. When they went farther afield, for
necessary shopping or to visit a doctor or dentist, they

either traveled in mutually protective pairs or were singly accompanied by a duenna, typically a pious-looking adolescent schoolgirl, usually named Mary Rose, Rita, or Regina, who appeared to be burdened equally with pride at having been chosen for this mission and responsibility for seeing that her charge came to no harm on the Lancaster sidewalks.

In social prestige, there was little to choose among the five Catholic parishes, but between the two synagogues there was considerable difference. Of the two, the Temple Shaarai Shomayim attracted the better-off Jewish families, tobacco merchants and wholesale dealers in dry goods as well as travel agents (the Goldens: their son Art was the smoothest dancer of my high school generation), dry cleaners (the Finkelsteins), cigar shop owners (the Steinfeldts), and fruit retailers (the Halperns). Although I had no occasion to observe any overt anti-Semitism in Lancaster, Jews were, I think, excluded from the Country Club and the downtown Hamilton Club. But they pulled their weight in the city's cultural and charity organizations, and in his participation in civic affairs the longtime head of their congregation, Rabbi Davis, set an example of mild ecumenism at a time when religious turfs were much more fixed than they subsequently became. The other synagogue in town, Degel Israel, whose typical member was a Russian-Jewish junk dealer, had no such standing. But even here, people were not irrevocably bound to their station in life: one junk dealer's daughter married a well-known young American poet.

In Lancaster there were no extremes of wealth or poverty. As elsewhere, there was a class structure, but in Lancaster it lacked a pinnacle. There were no grandees such as the Lilly family in Indianapolis, the Balls in Muncie, or the Wideners, Stotesburys, or Atwater Kents (radio-manufacturing wealth) on the rich outskirts of Philadelphia. The social gradations began at the top of the middle class and were manifested in such ways as the relative standing of the country clubs. The Lancaster Country Club, on the New Holland Pike just before you got to the little crossroads called Eden, was the oldest and most select, composed as it was of third- or fourth-generation city families (old money) and relative newcomers, industrialists and merchants with the right credentials (new money). The Meadia Heights Golf Club, on the other side of town on the Willow Street Pike, was for types subsequently known as Jaycees (Junior Chamber of Commerce), up-and-coming second-echelon businessmen who placed more store on the useful social contacts that membership provided than did the comparatively settled elite on the New Holland Pike. Back north, on the Lititz Pike, was Overlook, for the leftovers. Like Meadia Heights, it was physically as well as socially distant from "the" Country Club, by a matter of several miles.

The wealthiest people in Lancaster got their money from a number of sources apart from farm land, which was securely in the hands of the plain people. Some were executives in major local industries such as Armstrong

65

Cork (linoleum), Hamilton Watch, and Follmer-Clogg
(umbrellas). Others were department store owners or
newspaper publishers; a few were leading physicians and
surgeons; and some had agricultural ties, as grain or
cattle dealers (one of the latter, Frank Musser, who as a
young man had lost an arm in a trolley accident, was a
popular mayor in the early 1920s). Their way of life was
modest indeed if compared with that of the Philadelphia
plutocracy on the estates down the Main Line at the
same moment. They employed no more than two or three
servants, a domestic labor force that sometimes included
"Mennonite girls" as maids (some went back to the farm
and made good marriages, bringing their children for
their former employers to admire) or by "German girls,"
actually from Germany, in an *au pair* arrangement such
as was popular at the time. They drove Cadillacs, Lin-
colns, Packards, Buicks, and Pierce-Arrows (never
Rolls-Royces, which true Lancastrians, no matter how
much money they had in the Farmers' Trust Company,
would condemn as sheer arrogance).

The best families spent weeks in Atlantic City's great
hotels, the Chalfont-Haddon Hall, Traymore, Strand,
and Marlborough-Blenheim; this was called "going to the
shore," and entailed sending back boxes of salt water
taffy to their stay-at-home dependents. (The name was
never clear to me, because I detected no taste of salt
water.) They had summer places, sometimes deprecat-
ingly called cottages, along the New Jersey coast or in
New England, and in addition they often vacationed in
Florida or Bermuda or even in Europe, going over on

one of the White Star, Cunard, North German Lloyd, Hamburg American, or French liners that were famous in the glory days of transatlantic travel, the *Berengaria, Leviathan, Mauretania, Homeric, Majestic, Aquitania, Bremen, Europa, Normandie, Ile de France.* The postcards they sent from Europe by surface mail—there was, of course, no other—took only a week to arrive. The women bought their dresses at Lancaster's most fashionable shop, Mary Sachs's on East King Street, and if Mary Sachs did not have what they wanted, they made a day trip to Philadelphia's best stores or spent a couple of days in New York, canvassing Bonwit Teller, Best, and Saks Fifth Avenue.

So much I knew from everyday observation, as an outsider. The picture was filled out later when I came upon John O'Hara's novels, whose "Gibbsville," though actually Pottsville in the upstate coal country, was a recognizable near-facsimile of Lancaster in its country club-Mary Sachs manifestation. If the Jazz Age ever affected Lancaster, it was there, hip flasks and all. (I knew for a fact that Mr. Kauffman, a gardener by day— his blue sweat-stained suspenders and gray moustache linger in my memory, along with his penchant for "getting a talker on" when he stopped by our porch— moonlighted for his bootlegging son, delivering cases of booze at moderately moneyed people's back doors after dark.) If someone in a high social circle applied himself or herself too liberally to the bottle, he or she was shipped across the Susquehanna, to Dr. Crandall's sanitarium on the road from Wrightsville to York, to dry out. The extra-marital dalliance described by O'Hara may well have occurred in the country club set, but I was not in a position to know about it.

Most of Lancaster's families belonged to the middle-middle or lower-middle class. Their breadwinners were small businessmen, salesmen, bookkeepers, teachers, store clerks, skilled craftsmen like the Hamilton watchmakers. If O'Hara's picture of upper-class Gibbsville society was a true image of Lancaster's, John Updike's later picture of lower-middle-class life in Brewer was an equally faithful portrayal of Lancaster's. (Updike grew up in Shillington, just across the Lancaster-Berks county line, where his father was a school teacher. "Brewer" is Reading, the Berks County seat.) The social ambience of Harry ("Rabbit") Angstrom, the high-school basketball star, is in virtually every respect the ambience of most children who grew up in Lancaster between the wars, except that he would have been named Hollinger or Darrenkamp, not Angstrom.

Lancaster also had a working class, composed of machine tenders at factories like Armstrong's and the cotton and silk mills, truck drivers, and unskilled laborers of every description. At its bottom was the poor-white element that lived, along with Negroes (the designation "blacks" was many years in the future), in Lancaster's closest approximation of a slum, the Seventh Ward in the southeastern quadrant, on the way to the gas works and Lamparter's facility for converting dead horses into glue. These were the people who, when hard times came, were most immediately in need of help.

Before the advent of public welfare in the middle 1930s, they had to depend on charity such as was provided by the Salvation Army and the Water Street Rescue Mission, a locally funded enterprise that, like most of the sort, had a religious message to convey along with shelter, hot meals, and castoff clothing. Some churches, and the Elks and other lodges, also had modest charity programs. The poor house and the insane asylum for the indigent were still in business on the edge of town, on the East King Street slope that led to Witmer's Bridge over the Conestoga; their function as a disposal bin for the luckless, friendless, and/or witless was inadequately concealed under the euphemisms "county home" and "county hospital." It was characteristic of Lancaster County that these were largely self-sufficient in food, which came from an adjacent farm worked by aged or indigent field laborers.

Short of these institutions of last resort, there were several alternative ways of dealing with long-term poverty and old age. Orphan boys could be sent to the Industrial School at Hershey, the Stevens Trade School (next door to the poor house!), or the munificently endowed Girard College in Philadelphia. The Mennonite Church had a "home" for the elderly outside Neffsville, memorable, as most such places were, for the worn brown linoleum on the floors, the smell of furniture polish, the plainly furnished bedrooms, and bells ringing. The Masons maintained a comfortable establishment, the equivalent of today's fee-paying retirement home, at Elizabethtown, but it was not a charitable institution. In Lancaster, "decayed females of respectable station," to use the genteel English term, could find permanent refuge in the Long and Witmer Homes, typical examples of the small local endowed philanthropies that intervened before a needy woman's desperation threatened to curtail her respectability.

There was a small colored community made up of domestic servants and menial laborers. Its existence was officially acknowledged by the presence of a token black on the police force, Officer Lavender, whose name inspired jokes and whose mission, it was facetiously alleged, was to hold the lid down on Saturday night razor work in the Rockland Street disorderly houses. The Seventh Ward was the town's worst crime area, a circumstance not much mitigated by the Crispus Attucks settlement house, which most Lancastrians knew only by name and about which they cared not at all. A branch of the National Association for the Advancement of Colored People was founded only in the late 1930s.

Apart from a few blacks in high school who, I now realize, strove for invisibility, the only resident colored person I knew at all well was Jerry Wilson, chauffeur and yard man to a family whose garage was across the alley from our back yard, and husband of their cook, Fanny. Jerry's idiosyncrasy was a stutter that he sometimes put on for comic effect; otherwise he talked plainly enough, as when we made bets on the second Dempsey-Tunney fight. (I forget on what basis of incomplete knowledge we chose sides, or which man I favored, but I do know that in the event no money changed hands.)

When I worked at the Gulf station at Chestnut and Plum, I got to know a "nice, soft-spoken, middle-aged colored man"—such a condescending description, however well-meant, was normal at the time, and I do not hesitate to repeat it here as a scrap of historical evidence—who signed the charge slip "Ed Arrington" after I had serviced the Bayuk Cigar truck he drove up from Philadelphia once a week. I hope that his children, if he had children, made it in life, and that his grandchildren did even better. He was a nice man.

There was also a tiny representation of what we today call other minorities. Mrs. Colatta and Mr. Clerico sold fruit and resoled shoes, respectively; Mr. Kim, who made a great point of not being Japanese but Korean—as well he might, considering that the Japanese then tyrannously occupied his homeland—sold Oriental wares; and there was a Greek family named Stathopoulos, but I forget whether they ran a shoeshine parlor or the Red Rose Café, which served diner-type food.

Apart from hovering anti-Semitism and the inevitable bias against blacks, I cannot recall any serious racial or ethnic prejudices that, as it were, kept people in their respective places. Lancaster society as a whole, and perhaps chiefly the lower-middle class, had its frictions and personal frustrations and its possibly restrictive system of morals and practically unattainable ambitions, but in general it was both settled and fluid. Because few of its industries were unionized, labor had to depend for equitable wages and decent working conditions on the self-interested benevolence of its employers. Strikes were rare in Lancaster, and I doubt if those that occurred were very successful. Many people attributed the absence of tensions that could be found in bigger and more highly industrialized cities to the fact that Lancaster was a notably church-going community; the influential presence of religion tended to minimize social conflicts. (The other side of the coin was that most churches failed to recognize, or if they recognized, failed to do much about the inequities and injustices that were rife in America— even Lancaster—but came to the surface only with the New Deal.)

Perhaps Lancaster's egalitarian climate was best epitomized by the way people referred to those who served them in one capacity or another. I have no reason to believe that the civility of address practiced in my home was not widely prevalent. It was "Mr. McNamee," the genial letter carrier, who made two deliveries a day, "Mr. Stapf," the neighborhood butcher, and "Mr. Williamson," the equally genial manager of Renninger's Meat Market downtown (there was a difference between a butcher shop and a meat market), who wore the bloodied apron and straw hat of his trade and had served in the Canadian Army during the war. It was "Mr. Heim," the motorman on the Marietta Avenue trolley, who when he went on vacation sent postcards written in his small, neat hand to a streetcar-fixated little boy who liked to sit behind him on his one-man trolley and converse.

Not that civility, in that form, was universal. One spoke only of "Buzzy" Shultz, the maker of the best ice cream in town, who was reluctant to sell it, with the result that prominent citizens, including our family physician, had to go to the side door of his house and ring the bell, as if they wanted to get into a speakeasy. Whether they actually had to get down on their knees and plead for a quart of vanilla, I never heard. Nobody ever called the elderly Western Union night messenger with leather puttees, flowing bohemian artist's black tie, and flat feet, who was a familiar figure on Lancaster streets, anything but Norm. And under the circumstances, "Patent Leather Johnny" was the only appropriate name—though of course it was never spoken in his hearing—for the man with a specialized foot fetish, a case which Krafft-Ebing would have treasured. He indulged his delight not only on the streets but in church; he belonged, I think, to a well-known Lancaster family. The human scene in the Square was dominated by Harry (few knew his last name was Rabinowitz), an energetic news vendor with tousled hair and skin rendered leathery by daily exposure to the weather, who darted from one customer to another as the streetcars came and went. Once in a later year I saw him on the platform at the railroad station, emotionally embracing his son, on his way to a midwestern university. It was a tableau which, for the moment, seemed to say that the American dream was not so unattainable as might be thought.

73

WORKING AND LIVING

If the past lingered always in the Lancaster air, it had
the good fortune not to be polluted by modern industry.
Lancaster was a prosperous manufacturing town but,
whether by purpose or accident, it had little heavy
industry to load the air with smoke and unseen particu-
lates or, for that matter, to attract a labor force of
European immigrants as did the grimy steelmaking towns
of Coatesville, across the Chester County line, or Steel-
ton, on the road to Harrisburg. Better fewer industries,
the city fathers reckoned, than the wrong kind. The
Champion Blower and Forge Company and one or two
small ironworks were tolerated because they had been
there a long time and did, after all, help the economy.
But most of Lancaster's industrial workers were employed in "clean" establishments, many of which, like
the several printing firms (Science Press, Lancaster
Press, Wickersham Printing Company) that turned out
learned journals and monographs, required skilled labor. This mix of productive enterprises was scattered

across the city; there was no industrial quarter. Most of them occupied red brick buildings whose architecture was the very definition of drab utility. Not until RCA located a radio tube-making plant on New Holland Avenue in the 1940s did Lancaster have what might be called a designer factory, built according to the latest standards of physical attractiveness and internal efficiency.

A sure and simple test that differentiated native Lancastrians from outlanders, apart from the pronunciation of the name—natives said LANCaster, people like nonresident Pennsylvania Railroad trainmen tended to say LANcaster—was the niceties of industrial terminology. Locally, Armstrong's was always a plant, not a factory, while Hamilton was a factory, not a plant or a watch works. Works were places like the ones where Armstrong's made cork bottle stoppers as a sideline or Slaymaker's turned out padlocks.

Preeminent among Lancaster's industries was the sprawling complex of tall, important-looking buildings at the northwest corner of the city where cork imported from Spain was ground up, mixed with linseed oil, and pressed and baked into Armstrong's linoleum, whose magazine advertisements put Lancaster on the map from coast to coast. Armstrong was the vicinity's biggest nonagricultural employer, constantly expanding as Americans were putting more and more of their disposable income into furnishing their homes.

The freight cars on the Armstrong sidings received backbreaking rolls of linoleum in the latest decorative patterns; from Lancaster's second largest industry came products a single year's output of which would scarcely have filled a (well-insured) boxcar. Along two blocks of the Lincoln Highway (Columbia Avenue at that point) stretched the red-brick headquarters of the Hamilton Watch Company, site of the annual Christmas extravaganza of lights. The building, with an illuminated clock tower at each end, was separated from the street by several acres of hedge-enclosed private park, with a well-kept lawn, mature trees, a lily pond, and flower beds featuring spectacular cannas, which were floodlighted at the height of their season. Here hundreds of expert handworkers, aristocrats of labor as were the compositors and proofreaders at the printing establishments— some had come from Switzerland—made the famous "watch of railroad accuracy," a slogan that, if accuracy could somehow be equated with punctuality, bespoke the reputation American railroads then enjoyed. Hamilton too was a lavish magazine advertiser, later on network radio as well. How many cities of our size, Lancastrians could justifiably ask, were known from coast to coast as the homes of *two* brand-name products?

Unlike Armstrong's, which conducted daily tours of its multi-building spread, the watch factory was closed to the public. Another well-established industry, only a block away, was Slaymaker's lock works, which did not have to provide tours: its operations could be watched from the sidewalk in warm weather, when men and women were tending punch presses inside the open windows and one could hear the rattle of the metallic blanks as they poured down the chute.

Out along the railroad was the Stehli silk mill, whose blue lights and clatter of looms from open windows on a summer night alerted the Lancaster passengers on trains from Philadelphia that they were approaching the station. There was also a large cotton mill in town. Both were in Lancaster primarily because the Follmer-Clogg umbrella factory, said to be the biggest of its kind in the world, was also there, requiring silk and cotton cloth as well as the lacquered handles that were made in smaller work places nearby. (Lacquer had a tendency to ignite on the smallest provocation, and when it did, it was likely to burn the building down.) But this was one industry that, unlike Armstrong's and Hamilton, proved vulnerable to changing fashions. When people started not to carry umbrellas in the 1930s, it suffered as heavily as the men's hat industry did at the same time, and the looming factory was converted into a branch showplace and warehouse for Van Sciver, Philadelphia's largest furniture retailer. The silk and cotton mills were additionally the victims of new technology as rayon and nylon began to replace natural fibers.

One industry-leading Lancaster business that was not celebrated in its own town but whose products were sought after in Europe as well as the United States was the Hubley Manufacturing Company, whose modest plant somewhere near the railroad I cannot now visualize. Successfully competing with German manufacturers, Hubley produced small metal toys which I recently discovered have become classics in their specialized field. Surviving examples—toys of course never have enjoyed a high preservation rate—command high prices on the antiquarian hobbyist's market and are pictured in the standard books on the subject. I even once saw a display of them in the Musée des Arts Décoratifs in Paris.

As elsewhere in those decades, retail selling and services in Lancaster were still dominated by local interests. There were far more family-owned and -managed businesses than chain outlets, even though these were slowly proliferating and furnishing one more proof that the city was keeping abreast of the times. Downtown were Woolworth's, McCrory's, Grant's, and Kresge's variety stores, a Penney's and a Montgomery Ward's (but not a Sears Roebuck), a Schulte's tobacco shop, and Walgreen's, Liggett's, and Rexall drugstores, one of which, every so often, held a one-cent sale during which you could buy a pint of ice cream for thirty cents and another pint for a single penny. Out in the neighborhoods were several little (by comparison with later ones) A & Ps, with clerks behind the counter. The sole self-service grocery was in Garvin's redolent basement.

Facing Penn Square, and eventually occupying the entire southeastern side, was Watt and Shand's, a yellow brick and terra cotta four-story-plus-basement structure that attractively displayed every line of goods that a modern department store could conceivably carry, as might be inferred from the fact that it was familiarly called "the New York Store." It commanded universal respect in town because of the quality of the merchandise it sold and the service it offered; it lived up to its punning slogan, which I admired, "On the Square." One evidence

79

of its up-to-the-minute efficiency was its use of pneumatic tubes to send money to the cash desk: clerks at slightly laggard stores, like Penney's and the home-owned Leinbach's, dispatched the money in metal containers that rode on overhead wires to the money changer at the rear of the store.

Retail businesses like these contributed to the sense of community that was typical of Lancaster and, no doubt, of many other cities at the time. If you were shopping for clothing or furniture, for example, or making a deposit in a bank, you were waited upon by men and women whom you knew in other connections, as neighbors, fellow churchgoers, members of the same club or lodge, or parents of children who went to the same school your children attended. Far from being mere time-clock punchers, many of them were veritable institutions where they worked, having spent perhaps ten or twenty years in the same department, familiar faces—human landmarks—that added to the confidence with which you dealt with a store. Not so at Woolworth's, McCrory's and the rest, where jobs were ill paid and the labor turnover rapid.

Neighborhood stores, some of them at the same location and under the same ownership for generations, still prospered. Mr. Fritz's little grocery at First Street and South West End Avenue, catty-cornered across from the lock works, was the very prototype of a mom-and-pop business, with living quarters attached. When you went in for a quarter-pound of dried beef, Mr. Fritz would put his fists, knuckles down, on the wooden counter and say "Now," as if he had just finished serving a queue of ten customers—although in fact nobody else was in sight. He would turn the crank of a machine that passed the joint back and forth across the knife edge of a rotating disc, depositing the paper-thin pink slices on a piece of waxed paper, and ring up the modest transaction on a brass cash register with levered keys, which produced a business-like *chink* as the cash drawer flew open.

Smithgall's drugstore near the college was a somewhat larger enterprise, but it too was typical of the time and place. Physicians making their morning rounds of patients—nobody dreamed that this would become an extinct routine—would drop in to drink a cup of coffee at the soda fountain, pass the time of day with colleagues, and turn in prescriptions which Smithgall's would fill and duly deliver by automobile, at no extra charge. It was not there, I think, but at other drugstores that I noticed a legend running straight across the top of the show window: DRUGS, RUBBER GOODS, AND SUNDRIES. After a lifetime of searching, I have yet to discover a single sundry of any shape or size.

There were neighborhood barber shops, too, with their revolving red, white, and blue-striped poles outside, but I patronized Bransby's, the big one downtown. Mr. Bransby, the owner, a short man in his sixties with close-cropped gray hair, presided at the first chair to the right as you went in and took a number; he also collected your money as you went out. At peak times he had as many as eight barbers at work on what amounted to a tonsorial mass production line. When one finished

81

with a head and shook out his cloth he would call the number on the board in front, which Mr. Bransby kept current. In the back of the shop was a waiting room with hard benches and portions of the day's newspaper; on Friday afternoons and all day Saturday there were times when there was standing room only. Because of the volume of business he did, Mr. Bransby charged only thirty-five cents for a haircut, a dime or so below the going rate.

One of the best working places from which to observe the day-to-day flow of the town's affairs was a gas station, or, to adopt the preferred term in the industry, a service station. Station 481 of the Gulf Refining Company, at East Chestnut and North Plum Streets, was an ideal place to watch Lancaster life in its street-level manifestations. In the early 1930s it was a fairly new operation, with a snug office, an outdoor lift for grease jobs (lubrication services, if you spoke by the book), and seemingly acres of white concrete that had to be kept innocent of oil drippings and grease smears by frequent scrubbings with long-handled brushes and strong detergent powder. It was the one modest jewel in what was otherwise a dilapidated crown, a neighborhood of working-class row houses set flush with the sidewalk, insignificant little factories, automobile repair shops, and vacant lots fronted by billboards.

Nothing exciting ever happened there, except once when a streetcar rammed a truck at the intersection. Considerable damage to both vehicles, but no injuries.

The police never had any errands roundabout. Because the station was not on a highway, its trade was largely local. The major exception was a long-distance trucking firm, garaged next door, that had a contract to haul freight from New Brunswick, New Jersey, to the Armstrong plant. Its open-cabbed Macks were brutes to drive. On the Lincoln Highway they labored up Gap Hill and then hurtled down the other side, the drivers hoping against hope that the brakes were in good repair. Coming in to refuel late on a hot summer afternoon, the sweaty drivers in their greasy pants and soiled undershirts would climb wearily down and make a beeline for the water cooler while I climbed up, inserted the hose nozzle in the under-the-seat tank, climbed down again, and started cranking thirty or forty gallons into the truck's insatiable innards. (Gulf Refining, at that date, had not yet installed electric pumps. Every gallon we delivered was pumped by hand.)

A gas station like ours succored men and women irrespective of class. The president of a local bank would come in in his Lincoln, bringing disillusion for a youth not yet fully conversant with the anomalies of life—for he was usually cuddling a large wad of tobacco in his cheek, and although this might have been permissible, and even to be expected, for a small-town banker out in the county, in my view it did not harmonize with the status of *his* bank, just across from the courthouse downtown. However, chew or no chew, his money house weathered the Depression, which was more than could be said for other banks in town; furthermore, once when

I checked his tires he gave me the unprecedented tip of fifty cents. Tips were rare in those days, and they seldom amounted to more than a dime.

While Mr. Newhouser was buying premium ethyl for his Lincoln, at another pump, which dispensed an inferior grade of motor fluid that had a more than superficial resemblance to kerosene, might be parked the rattletrap Ford truck of an ebullient young colored man named Wright, who had a firewood route. He usually bought a single gallon of gas at a time with high and humorous ceremony, but on weekends, if he planned to go out on the town, he might up the order to an extravagant two.

The truck drivers who worked out of the garage next to the station were a rough and tough lot; they had to be, to stand the rigors of jockeying those primitive Macks. Several of them lived in the neighborhood, and for one of them, Bill Nixdorf, I once acted as amanuensis. It was the period of the NRA (National Recovery Agency), and Bill strongly suspected that his employers were not living up to the regulations prescribed in the NRA's fair practice code for long-distance truckers. One evening he came to me with a letter of complaint he proposed to send to the President of the United States. He wanted me, an educated person (a college freshman), to polish it up for him and type the final version on the typewriter in the station office. I succeeded in making his letter more intelligible and even, perhaps, a bit more forceful, while at the same time preserving the genuine flavor of Bill Nixdorf. Naturally, I retained the opening paragraph in which he reminded Mr. Roosevelt that the

Nixdorfs had named their newly born twins Franklin and Eleanor. The succeeding bill of particulars was fired by the same spirit of indignation that pervaded the addresses the American colonies made to the government of George III. When Bill was satisfied that I had captured all the nuances of his intention, I typed off several copies, one of which Bill sent to a local newspaper, where it promptly appeared.

I never heard whether Mr. Roosevelt or General Hugh Johnson, head of the controversial NRA, replied, or what view Bill's employers took of his breaking into print, and what is more, getting into personal touch with Washington. I imagine they were not amused. But I am still bothered a little about the ethics of my having used a typewriter belonging to the company headed by Andrew Mellon, the rock-ribbed Republican multimillionaire who was secretary of the treasury under Harding, Coolidge, and Hoover, to compose and disseminate a document so full of rebellious passion.

At least half the actors on the stage at Chestnut and Plum were not paying customers. They were simply the people of the neighborhood who, especially in the evenings, made the Gulf property a hangout as customarily as, in an earlier era, they had gravitated to the corner cigar store or saloon. This, said The Company—that distant, mysterious, arbitrary, despotic authority represented locally by a district manager who, like all such supervisory lackeys the country over, was called The Old Man—was Strictly Out of Order. (I am quoting.) But there was little their employees could do about it, short of making their little offices over into the semblance of armed fortresses.

Mary, a plain fifteen-year-old girl who lived across the street, made several trips a day in warm weather to fill a large glass pitcher with ice water from our electric cooler. I think we supplied most of the neighborhood with ice water. Gus the cop parked his motorcycle out of the way and retired to the back room for a quiet smoke and a perusal of the latest issue of the funny paper the company was distributing at that time as a promotional scheme. (The appearance of a new issue would attract hordes of clamorous kids, none of whom was in a position to buy even a pint of gasoline.) Uncle Rudy, a pot-bellied, sixtyish man with suspenders, five-and-ten-cent store glasses, and no known occupation, wandered in to report to me the scores of the baseball games played at dusk in the county league, intelligence in which I was supremely uninterested. If, by any chance, I seemed extra-hospitable, he would linger to give me graphic descriptions of executions he had witnessed as a young man. The most sensational hanging ever to take place in town, he told me more than once with touching regret, he had missed; the night before, he had got drunk, and when the trap was sprung in the county jailyard he was sleeping off his jag in a shack behind the gas works. I think I took this in without the slightest skepticism; I now suspect that Uncle Rudy was fibbing. In the first place, although convicted criminals were hanged locally well within his lifetime, executions were not public spectacles; in the second place, the story about missing the great moment because of incapacitation crops up time after time in the lore of public hangings. Uncle Rudy may well have been one of those key figures in the history of folklore, the transmitter of a myth to a new generation.

The three brothers, Chick, Beanie, and Frank, gay young blades who lived in a tatty block of flats across the street, drifted in to debate, over paper cups of ice water, whether they should go out to an amusement park or spend the evening in a beer joint nearer home. Joe Tammany, the white-haired barber who for forty years had been running a one-chair shop in a little white building on the other side of our fence to the east (the truck terminal was to the north), stopped on his way home to polish his pince-nez glasses and reminisce about the days when there were fields in this vicinity, and nothing but a stable down on the next block and the streetcar barn at the end of the street.

Even those regular passersby who never made our office a port of call were well known to me. There was, for instance, the vendor of warm crabcakes who came down the street, a big white-covered basket on his arm, giving his cry as if he were in Porgy and Bess' Catfish Row rather than in the midst of Pennsylvania Dutch land. "Lady walked all the way down from Columbia [nine miles away] to buy some this morning," he often boasted. Then there was the enigmatic swarthy man known to us only as Cigar, who took the short cut through our driveway four times a day, following the long unlighted stogie he always had in his mouth and

87

never looking to right or left. He was rumored to be a foreigner, a well-paid tool designer or something in a tin can factory down the street, but we never did establish this with certainty. Down the sidewalk across the street, at irregular intervals day and night, strode a frowsy character known as The Old Dutchwoman, who lived in what was reputed to be the dirtiest hovel in the neighborhood. She was somewhat bent, and as she walked she made frequent grabs at the small of her back, the popular, and plausible, explanation being that she had bugs in her clothing. She was perpetually searching for Goldie, supposedly her granddaughter, a most unattractive adolescent who was said to be the worst of the bad lot who infested the Dutchwoman's house.

It will be seen from this that those who worked the late afternoon and evening shift never lacked companionship. But when I was on that shift, alone, I had other plans for my eight hours. Normally, except for the rush at the dinner hour when people were gassing up for their evening's adventures, the shift wasn't particularly busy. Moreover, the two day men did most of the maintenance work around the premises, so there wasn't much for me to do but wait on such trade as did come in. Those hours were too precious to be wasted on eternal chit-chat with the casual droppers-in, however much light it might sometimes shed on the inexhaustible subject of how other people lived. So while I don't think I was ever actually inhospitable, I didn't encourage unlimited hanging around. What I really wanted to do was read. It was at this gas station that I first discovered and exploited the advantages of an occupation that allowed one to read books while being paid for nominally working. I have been reading on the job ever since.

There was, however, this (temporary, as it happily proved) fly in the ointment: Clarence Hickey, a big, blond, hairy-chested station manager, was an enemy of literature. For a gas station manager, he had a perfectly tumultuous psyche. His father, whom he seldom saw, was reputedly a choleric Irish grocer and lord of an obscure manor named Sunnyside, hardly more than a weed-grown shanty town, on the outskirts of Lancaster not far from the glue works. Clarence had had no family life to speak of as a child; as he expressed it to me more than once, in his confidential mood, his innate yearning for love had been "stiffled."

Somehow he had been converted to Catholicism—a rather spectacular leap from the United Brethren denomination, though how a family named Hickey had become United Brethren in the first place puzzled me— and he took his religion seriously. In the midst of a busy Saturday afternoon at the station, he would suddenly knock off to go over to St. Anthony's, two blocks away, for confession. What with confession and the subsequent acts of penance (the stiffer the penance allotted to him, the happier he was) he was away for the rest of the afternoon. When he came back to knock off for the day, his new state of spiritual asepsis was evident chiefly in the added pungency of his vocabulary. Even when most engulfed in unshriven sin, his command of profanity was always at least equal to that of the truck drivers, but when his soul was cleansed his way of putting things achieved an almost unearthly, however shocking, splendor. After work on Saturdays he would go to his boarding house—he rented a room from a pudgy-faced, slovenly organist at one of the Catholic churches who drove a rusty car with windows smeared by the slobberings of several beagles riding in the back seat—clean up, and embark on a career of indulgence appropriate to his big frame and fairly elemental appetites. The next morning his lusty baritone would lead all the rest in St. Anthony's choir.

Hickey's only idols, the more so because they led sanctified lives unattainable to him because of his lack of schooling, were religious professionals, if I may call them such, and it was a great hour at the station when a parish priest drove in to have his car serviced. Only Hickey in person could do the honors on such an occasion, and as he scrubbed the clerical windshield and checked the battery water as if it were in a baptismal font, he threw in all the "Yes Fathers" and "No Fathers" the conversation could bear. He was beside himself when, as happened once in a while, a big black chauffered sedan containing two or three nuns pulled in. In those moments Hickey's life came to momentary, ecstatic fulfillment. During slack hours in the station, he loved to relive his informal contacts with the priests at the various churches he had attended; to him a half-hour's social call at a rectory meant what a cozy visit in the White House might have meant to other people, possibly including Bill Nixdorf. He would reproduce the entire conversation, innocently attributing to the priests the same earthy vigor of language that distinguished his own.

When we went about our maintenance chores, white-washing the curbs of the pump islands, polishing the brasswork, or giving the pumps a fresh coat of paint, we made music. The laity among us usually drew our songs from the repertory of the "Lucky Strike Hit Parade" on the radio, but not Hickey. He bellowed forth, instead, the Latin hymns he had learned in the choir. As he had not gone beyond grade school, I doubt if he knew the meaning of a single Latin word, but that did not faze him; indeed, it probably added to his enjoyment, since from the beginning of the race, we are told, unintelligi-bility has had a rare mystic beauty all its own.

It was not inconsistent with Hickey's complicated per-sonality that he should also have been a flower lover. The company was delighted to have him raise petunias and marigolds in green boxes ranged around the station property, and he watered them as devotedly as he said his rosary. Once or twice I detected him furtively dipping water out of his sprinkling can and making the gesture over the flowers that one associates with a priest and his aspergillum, all the while singing a "Kyrie Eleison" with the fullthroatedness that other men reserved for a drink-ing song.

Hickey, however, was, as I have said, the enemy of secular reading in any form. On one of the first days I worked for him, I incautiously pulled out a book when business was slack. "Put that damn book away!" he bellowed. "I'm not goin' to have any book-readin' around here!" I scuttled back to my locker and put the book away, and conceived for Clarence Hickey a temporary fierce hostility such as Browning's malevolent monk harbored against the pious Brother Lawrence:

> Gr—r—r— there go, my heart's abhorrence!
>   Water your damned flower-pots, do!
> If hate killed men, Brother Clarence,
>   God's blood, would not mine kill you!

But I soon found out, by experiment, that if I sneaked my book into the station inside a large manila envelope, which might just as well have contained sandwiches, nobody would be the wiser. Once Hickey left for the day, he was not likely to return, except after his Saturday shriving, and if the Old Man happened to turn up in his company Ford on a snooping expedition, I could always slip the book under the desk.

And so, thanks to the fact that I frequently worked the late shift in a gas station that did most of its business during the daylight hours, I managed to get a great deal of reading done in the summers I spent there. I might boast that I am the only gas station attendant on record who read portions of Xenophon in the original Greek while on duty, and I would be stating the literal truth (I actually was taking a course in elementary Greek), but this was merely a stunt, performed for the sake of including it in a book I was going to write many years later.

The five o'clock whistles blew at the factories around

town, Hickey went, and I felt a sudden joyful sense of emancipation. The sun set behind the row of old houses across the street, and the expanse of concrete, which had baked all day in the summer sun, began to cool. I took off the sun glasses I had been wearing, emptied the refuse baskets in the rest rooms, and looked idly through the pile of credit slips to see which of our regular customers had been in during the day shift. Perhaps Agnes Moedinger came in—a physical education teacher in a junior high school, who, learning of my interest in books, once lent me her book-club copies of Stefan Zweig's *Marie Antoinette* and Marcia Davenport's *Mozart* to read during my evening vigils—and I serviced her Chrysler roadster, never dreaming that within a year or two she would be killed in that car, in a collision at a city intersection.

At twilight I snapped on the dozen switches that controlled the station's lighting system and settled myself at the desk with my book. Trade would not be neglected; even with both eyes fixed on the page before me, my ear would tell me if anybody pulled into the driveway. Propping my right leg, heavy in regulation leather puttee, on the edge of an open drawer, I leaned back in my steel chair. Not absolutely solid comfort, but it would do; not even the occasional drop of ice water that ran down my neck from the faucet behind me was seriously discommoding. The belt line trolley car ground across the intersection every ten minutes or so, somewhere a radio played, once in a while one of the Mack trucks strained up Plum Street at the beginning of a long night's journey to New Brunswick. But these noises were so familiar that I would have been lost without them, and otherwise the neighborhood was peaceful. The smell of gasoline and oil faded away, and I acquainted myself, for the first time, with a catholic company of writers: George Gissing, Walt Whitman, G.K. Chesterton, E.M. Forster . . . to Don Marquis ("archy and mehitabel").

I also conceived a passion for Max Beerbohm, than whom no other author could have been further removed in spirit from a gas station in a southeastern Pennsylvania Dutch city. So overwhelmed was I by the exquisitely polished style of his essay "In Defence of Cosmetics," in a volume I had borrowed from the public library, that I decided to copy it out. It had been a hot July day, and in the evening a most terrific thunderstorm developed, which seemed to stall directly over our corner. The brilliant lightning bolts were accompanied by instantaneous crashing thunder, and sparks flew from the electric outlets in the office; every moment I was sure the next bolt would choose my typewriter for its target. But I kept typing stolidly on, and when the master fuse blew, casting everything into darkness, I simply propped up a flashlight over the desk and continued to commune with the incomparable Max.

On a less heroic occasion, I spent an evening of solid happiness whose memory I still cherish. For three days the rain had been pelting down, and on this, the fourth day, it was coming down harder than ever, driven by a gale some said came from a hurricane on the coast. I had the late shift by myself, and after the day men left,

I battened down the hatches more securely and prepared
to ride out the storm. My heavy oilskin hung dripping
and sticky on the mouthpiece of the pay telephone; for
mute companions I had heavy brass fire extinguishers,
which normally should have been attached to wall brack-
ets outside, but which now stood in a row on the office
floor for the sake of keeping untarnished. The day had
been so dark that night brought scarcely any change.
The rain dashed against the office windows and ran in
floods down the driveway, and Hickey's petunias were a
sorry sight. On the corner of the property the big
illuminated Gulf sign, shaped like an inverted banjo,
swayed in the gale.

This was a night for Conrad or Richard Henry Dana
or even Melville; but at the time I happened to be
treating myself to a course of reading in theatrical
reminiscences, and the library book I had brought along
was Augustus Thomas's long since forgotten *The Print of
My Remembrance*. All I remember of it now is one or two
anecdotes, but it will always be linked with the snug
comfort of that night. The city street lights were out of
commission, and all I could see beyond the station itself
were the dim oblongs of windows in the apartment house
across the street, and the twin headlight beams of some
cautious car groping its way through the torrent. Nobody
came in for gas, and nobody came in to loaf. The only
visitors I had were several distressed mariners who came
in to beg a spot of kerosene with which to anoint the
spark plugs of their stalled cars. After the first two or
three of these interruptions, I set a gallon can of kero-

sene outside the door, and when the next dripping unfortunate appeared out of the tempest I simply jerked my thumb in the direction of the can.

The sturdy brick office rode the storm well. The water cooler hummed awhile and then fell thoughtfully silent; at intervals the compressor in the back room set up a din, chugging to manufacture the free air that nobody wanted on a night like this. The Gulf Refining Company lost money that night. It would have done better to abandon the station to the elements and thus save both my wages and the cost of the electricity I used. But I am still grateful to it for giving me such a memory.

Years later, I discovered on reading James T. Farrell's once-admired trilogy of novels of proletarian Chicago life that ten years earlier, he — and in turn his ill-fated hero, Studs Lonigan—also worked at a gas station. Obviously, there was a world of difference between a Sinclair gas station on Chicago's tough South Side and a Gulf one in the comparative serenity of a neighborhood in Lancaster, Pennsylvania. Still, Farrell, Studs, and I had the experience in common. I have often wondered what Studs read; if he read anything at all, I doubt that it was Max Beerbohm.

It was part of the Pennsylvania Dutch legend, believed in most implicitly by people far removed from the scene, that Lancaster County people ate heartily. In this department of life there was no room, even among the Amish, for austerity; witness the number of dishes that were said to be specialties of their farmhouse kitchens:

snitz un knep (sliced applies cooked with large dough balls), shoofly pie (molasses pie with sugar crumbs on top), pot cheese (with the color and consistency of Camembert), scrapple (ground pork mixed with meal), and that wonderful treat, available only on Shrove Tuesday, fastnachts. These were deep-fried crullers with crisp surfaces that could be either dipped in powdered sugar or liberally coated with molasses. My grandmother's output on that day was always completely spoken for, by neighbors, in advance.

What these Pennsylvania Dutch eatables lacked in French delicacy—though no Frenchman would have scorned fastnachts—they made up for in sheer heartiness. Eventually the legend would spread so widely that restaurants as far west as Iowa would advertise "Pennsylvania Dutch food." Some of it, an *echt* Lancastrian never heard of; some, bearing a familiar name, he wouldn't recognize, let alone eat. The notion that a "typical" Pennsylvania Dutch dinner consisted of seven sweets and seven sours is a myth.

The abiding evidence of the dimensions and demands of the Lancastrian stomach was the farmers' indoor markets, half a dozen of them in the early twenties but two alone, the Central and Southern only a block apart, surviving into the forties. These were large municipally owned warehouse-like buildings whose several wide aisles were lined with stalls tenanted twice weekly, Tuesday afternoon/Wednesday morning and Friday afternoon/Saturday morning, by farmers and butchers and their wives and daughters who "came in" to town, first by horse-

97

drawn conveyances and later by car or truck. (The Amish, as I have said, had to depend on others for their transportation when it became impracticable to drive into the city.) The black market wagons were essentially commercial versions of Amish buggies, passenger space giving way to commodities. I have dim memories of rows of such vehicles backed up to the curb on both sides of the first block of East King Street, their empty shafts— the horses having been removed to nearby stables— raised in the air like the ceremonial sword-raising that salutes a bride and groom emerging from a church after a military wedding. The wagons had top-hinged tailgates, and when these were propped up, the vendors set up tables under them and sold their wares on the sidewalk.

But these open-air markets posed too much of a traffic problem, and by the late twenties all the trade was carried on indoors. Displayed on the plain wooden counters, under a simple sign giving the occupants' names and villages or R.F.D. numbers, was a great variety of home-produced commodities: fancy work, potting plants, cut flowers (peonies as big as cabbages), and above all, a cornucopia of food: meats, cheeses, vegetables, fruit, jellies, home-baked bread, pies, cakes, potato chips. . . . Lancaster city women and even some men, carrying capacious wicker baskets, would move from counter to counter, some stopping at stands they regularly patronized—Ira Herr for red meats, Lowry's for pork, Sam Shaeffer's for cheese—while others shopped around to find the best prices. The standard approach was "What are your berries today?"—or eggs or beans or peaches or lettuce or asparagus or tomatoes or beets. The answer being delivered by the prayer-capped Mennonite woman presiding over her display of bunches and boxes, the shopper might select a particular bunch or box, or she might wander on, index finger placed against pursed lips in an attitude of judicious consideration.

Little Amish boys and girls, brought along to help out, got an early taste of what would in due time become their own way of making a living. (Some stalls, rented by the year, were passed down from generation to generation, like subscription seats at the Philadelphia Orchestra.) A man who grew horseradishes shed tears as he fed those fiery white roots into a mechanical grinder; customers would take the product home in little waxed-paper cornets, add vinegar, and have themselves a condiment as potent as Indian curry. It was a scene almost worthy of a Breughel. It had happened twice a week for a century or more, and when people came from elsewhere, on business or to visit, it was the one city attraction they had to see.

Some food products were still brought to the door of a Lancaster home. Bakers, milkmen, and, in season, ice men had their regular routes, and for a long time they continued to use horse-drawn wagons; one dairy, indeed, kept its wagons on the streets until well into the Second World War, an anachronism that paid off when gasoline was rationed. Because automobiles—"machines," as they were sometimes called by older people — were becoming more and more common, it was a novel experience for a child to be allowed to climb onto the driver's seat of a bakery wagon, in proximity to the horse's sleek brown rump, and hold the reins: as much fun as sitting behind the wheel of a touring car and pretending to steer it while imitating the sound of the horn: *ga-doo-gah*! On one occasion, the ice man tethered his horse to an apple tree in our back yard, and I posed, aged seven or so, on the animal for a snapshot. Just why the horse was led there, I haven't the slightest notion; it was certainly not for the specific sake of what much later, and in a very different context, would be called a photo opportunity.

The horse-drawn wagons had followings. Mrs. Seaber, a couple of doors up the street, was always on the lookout when the milkman was due, and if she was lucky the horse would oblige; whereupon, she put on her gray gardening sunbonnet, took a small shovel, and appropriated the fresh deposit. It made incomparable compost, as every Amish farmer knew. In summer, kids would follow the ice wagon around and grab shards of lickable ice that resulted when the man expertly chopped the right size of cake (ten cents, twenty cents) for the customer's refrigerator. They envied his strength as he encompassed the cake with a pair of big tongs and half-walked, half-ran with it into the kitchen. This was an occupation that came into the unaccustomed limelight when the newspapers reported that the great football hero of the time, Red Grange, kept in summer shape by lugging ice.

Close as it was to the Chesapeake Bay and the Atlantic, Lancaster enjoyed a good variety of fresh seafood. In the basement of the North Market House at Queen and Walnut was Mettfett's fish market, which had a small seafood bar where downtown businessmen could drop in for a plate of fried oysters or a bowl of oyster stew. Kegel's on West King Street, still in business the last I knew, ran a popular restaurant in addition to its over-the-counter trade. And somewhere on Cabbage Hill—I don't know why I had to walk all that distance with my lidded agate pail, as if I were rushing the growler to a neighborhood saloon—was an establishment that sold succulent oysters, the big kind you had trouble swallowing one at a time, in thick broth. A pailful of two- or three-centers made a good meal for a small family. During a short season in the early spring, the shad ran in the Bay, providing Lancaster with its one undoubted gourmet delicacy, the sweetest and tenderest of all Eastern fish with great pockets of roe.

Another local specialty, though nobody claimed gourmet status for it, was the pretzel. The hard kind, liberally coated with coarse salt in order, it was said, to stimulate thirst for the beer it was intended to accompany, was made by hand in several small bakeries in Lancaster and the Moravian town of Lititz eight miles to the north. Not until much later would a machine be developed that bent the long strips of dough into the peculiar pretzel shape, and so this was a highly labor-intensive industry. Comedians made jokes about pretzel bending as if it were a mythical occupation, but people who went to Hammond's or Anderson's or Sturgis's bakeries to buy a pound or two warm from the oven knew differently: there, at long tables, sat women who did nothing but bend pretzels all day long. Pretzels were also good to eat with homemade ice cream, which was churned, also by hand, in wooden tubs, the metal container with the basic ingredients of milk and flavoring (strawberries or peaches in season) surrounded by a freezing combination of fragmented ice and salt. Soft pretzels, larger in size and intended to be eaten with a dash of mustard, were vended in the downtown streets, as they were in Philadelphia, but I never acquired a taste for them.

Because relatively few women worked outside the home, most Lancaster eating was done *en famille*. Restaurants played a small role in everyday life except on special occasions, when a family party might go for dinner to one of the city's two major hotels, the Brunswick or the Stevens House, or the Weber, which was a bit inferior. (The other Lancaster hotels, the Lincoln, the Milner, and the Lancaster itself, were fleabags, their dark cuspidor-equipped lobbies tenanted by seedy men who might have been pensioners or down-at-the-heel traveling salesmen. Willy Loman patronized a higher grade of hostelry.) The Sunday morning church set went, after service, to the popular cafeteria in the Y.M.C.A., where the college-age son of the minister of one of the Reformed churches, untroubled by Sabbatarian scruples, presided at the cash register. During the week, downtown workers had several restaurants to choose from at noon. There was one called Delmonico's in an old building on the Square, which disappeared when renovators converted the premises into an Arrow Shirt shop; I never ate there nor did I ever hear of anyone who did, but it is fair to assume that the menu never measured up to the name. My own preference was for the thirty-five-cent hot roast beef sandwich, with mashed potatoes and gravy, that could be had at the lunch counter in Watt and Shand's basement. But even this was nothing compared with the tender-crusted hot beef pie (and chocolate whipped cream cake for dessert) that you could get by pushing coins into slots alongside the appropriate windowed compartments in one of Philadelphia's Horn and Hardart ("Less work for mother") automats.

After the movies, drugstores were the place to go to prolong the pleasure. There were three of them on the west side of the second block of North Queen Street: Miller's (which was said to be some sort of relative of the one in New York's Pennsylvania Station, though I never got the connection straight), Cooper's, and the Imperial. The layout in all three was the same: soda fountain in front, prescription dispensary in the rear, and in between, little round glass-topped tables with an open cylinder of drinking straws on top, and beneath the glass a few boxed items of toiletries. The chairs with wrought iron backs and legs were adequate for the time required to leisurely absorb a soda or a sundae but not so comfortable as to tempt one to linger indefinitely. On the walls were glass cases displaying a further assortment of perfumes, lotions, and cosmetics. If there is any such thing as an association transposed from one sense to another, my memory of those hospitable drugstores is

103

preserved in an imaginary odor suggested by a combination of the cool hard marble of the soda fountain and the dark brown viscous syrup that topped the chocolate ice cream sundaes along with a sprinkling of nuts.

In the late 1930s, the most popular spot for either an après-show soda or a full meal was a restaurant called the German Village, which was that American rarity, then as now, a high-toned bus station. For a long time, Lancaster had had to cope with the intercity (Philadelphia to Pittsburgh) buses, Greyhounds plus several now extinct species such as Yelloways and Nevinses, that used the curb on heavily traveled North Queen Street as a place to set down and pick up passengers. To remove the nuisance, a group of businessmen built nearby a proper terminal, loading bays and all, with access to an alley for the buses, and attached to it a full-service restaurant and cocktail lounge. The terminal itself withered away, however, when the opening of the Pennsylvania Turnpike drew the intercity bus traffic from the Lincoln Highway, and after some years the German Village disappeared as well.

In summer there were outdoor church festivals with fresh strawberries, either intact (served with sugar) or in the form of ice cream or juicily layered in a sponge cake. These festivals were mostly an urban type of fund raiser; out in the country, the volunteer fire departments, eternally striving to pay off the mortgages on their engine houses or buy a new fire truck, put on genuine Pennsylvania Dutch spreads featuring chicken corn soup, another regional dish: the eastern Pennsyl-

vania counterpart of the scallop and crab dinners that
were part of summer life on Cape Cod.

As more and more cars took to the road, restaurants
sprang up alongside. On the Lincoln Highway at Paradise
an old stone tavern was converted into a popular restaurant called The Willows; it was nothing if not respectable. For the faster set, the place of choice was Obie
Miller's, which was one of those so-called road houses
that were not on a main road at all but discreetly hidden
on a back one, in this case "off the Oregon [Ephrata?]
Pike." Road houses generally had a dubious reputation
at that time as rural speakeasies, the name suggesting
dim lights, a furtive air, and the possible imminence of a
raid. It was where the more sporty fraternity brothers
at the college took their dates, and to Lancaster percep-
tions, that was, in the language of the time, nuff said.
But it probably wasn't all that bad. Obie Miller's steaks
were widely said to be very good. But they couldn't have
excelled the ones served, almost off the hoof, at the
Stock Yards Hotel, just across the Lititz Avenue railroad
bridge and adjacent to the stock yards themselves.

As I have already noted, during Prohibition Lancastrians who could afford it had their dependable sources
of alcoholic supply. Those with smaller advantages had
to make their own. Gin may have been made in Lancaster
bathtubs, but of this I have no knowledge. Beer, which
was more to the German taste, could be brewed at home,
but here again memory fails. I do know that it was
possible to make *root* beer in large dishpans, with ex-
tract, yeast, sugar, and water, and bottle the product

105

for fermentation and later consumption. Once in a while, the cap on a bottle stored, according to instructions, in a cool place in the cellar, gave way, and the resultant *pop* was an embarrassment when there was company in the living room.

What with its honest, nourishing food, its clean air, and the overall safety of its industries, Lancaster was a healthy place to live. Conventional wisdom also maintained that if one had to get sick, there was no better place to do it. Along with two hospitals and a small tuberculosis sanitarium, Lancaster abounded with good physicians and surgeons. Some, like the Atlee family, who dated back almost to colonial times, were dynasts, distinguished son following distinguished father in the profession. Others, graduates of such eminent Philadelphia medical schools as the University of Pennsylvania, Jefferson, and Hahnemann, may have been attracted to the city by their presence. More than a few doctors, born elsewhere, had taken their pre-med training at Franklin and Marshall and had become so much attached to Lancaster that they returned to set up their practice there. Among them were pioneers in their fields: one Lancaster physician was among the nation's first allergists, and a Lititz dentist broke ground in the new field of orthodontia.

The leading society physician, Dr. Prizer, wore a neatly trimmed beard that reminded people of England's George V, and drove his Ford coupe with dignity. He and his colleagues gave Lancastrians great confidence in their profession. But when orthodox medicine failed to cure, there were also osteopaths to consult, and when they failed, recourse could be had to chiropractors. As a last resort, even Dr. Prizer's patients, Country Club people, might make stealthy trips up to Cabbage Hill, where someone they called "the pow-wow woman" practiced. From such stray mentions of her as I overheard, I could not quite ascertain what curative strategies she employed; seemingly she "did," whatever that meant—I envisioned her as an old crone, pronouncing esoteric formulas over the sufferer. And I may not have been wrong, considering the locale; after all, if one believed the lore of ignorant outsiders (there was no truth to it), the famous hex signs on Pennsylvania Dutch barns and sewed into quilts were meant to keep witches away, and maybe she hexed people in a beneficial manner.

Children's contagious diseases were more prevalent than they would become with the introduction of preventive shots, and physicians had to report such cases to the Board of Health, whereupon a man would come around to the house and tack up alongside the door a cardboard quarantine notice, individual colors for scarlet fever, mumps, measles, whooping cough, chicken pox, and diphtheria. Theoretically this barred from the house visitors who would spread the contagion, but the warnings were largely unheeded and eventually the placards went out of use.

So too did that other token of domestic distress, the somber wreath on the door that announced that the body of a man, woman, or child was lying in a casket in

107

the living room, whose shades were drawn or shutters closed and the familiar furniture either disarranged or removed—an unnecessary contribution to the emotional stress that bereavement entailed. The solemnity of the occasion was deepened by the almost palpable scent of "funeral flowers" in the small unventilated space. From the house, the funeral procession moved to a church, and from there to one of Lancaster's several cemeteries, the proceedings all under the experienced supervision of Frederick F. (Freddy) Groff, the doyen of local morticians, who saw to the final rites for more Lancastrians than any of his several competitors. Cremations were seldom desired, so that the undertakers with their selections of luxurious caskets and their elegantly ornamented black hearses prospered.

But slowly it came about that the casket no longer occupied the living room but was open to view at announced hours in the "funeral home," where services were often held in lieu of a church. This was one of the many changes in social custom, most of them imperceptible because they were so gradual, that affected Lancaster life between the wars. The installation of electricity in homes was almost completed when I was a very young child: I can barely remember the gas fixtures, with their incandescent globes, that preceded the wiring of our house. Slowly disappearing, too, as new houses were being built and older ones converted to heating oil, were the delivery trucks of coal merchants like Houser and Coho and (with a distinctive checkerboard livery) W.W. Heidelbaugh. Until then, Lancaster's furnaces had burned anthracite ("hard") coal, which was odorless and smokeless; it came in three sizes for domestic use, pea, nut, and egg. A characteristic sound of the city began to be heard less frequently, that of a ton or two of coal rattling down a metal chute from the truck, across the sidewalk, into a house's basement. The grimy driver either shoveled it by hand, in a rudimentary rhythm (first the shovel biting into the coal, then the rattle), or uptilted the bed of the truck, opened a sliding vent at the rear, and let the whole load course down the chute in a continuous clattering stream, leaving a coating of coal dust on the pavement or snow.

When the fuel oil trucks arrived, coal men found their occupation dissolving beneath them. An earlier casualty on the streets was the rag man, who drove a broken-down cart pulled by a spavined horse and uttered a (to me) unintelligible cry. It was to this unkempt, vaguely menacing figure that Lancaster grandmothers threatened to consign little children as an irrevocable penalty for some trifling offense.

Inside the home, the very process of telephoning was being revolutionized. Upright instruments, with receivers on hooks, replaced the old boxes on the wall, which I remember only in old-fashioned business places. Telephones on the same party line bore a common number (ours was 132) but were differentiated by letter, J, M, R, W. When you wanted to call a neighbor, you had to ask the operator ("central") to "ring W on the line"—that would have been the Weavers, up the street—, hang up, and listen to the rings until the neighbor answered and they stopped.

ENJOYING

Populated as the surrounding county was by thousands
of strict sectarians who disapproved of any kinds of
modern amusement, one would think that Lancaster was
a dull and depressing place to grow up, a kind of moral
prison house. I read the books of Mencken and Sinclair
Lewis, and I was inclined to share their view that puri-
tanism brooded widely and darkly over the American
scene, hamstringing the wholesome pursuit of happiness.
But I could not honestly say that it applied to Lancaster
with more than usual force, even if the Amish and
Mennonite meeting houses in the country proclaimed it
to be spiritually, if not geographically, located squarely
in the middle of the Bible Belt. The wowsers, as Mencken
called them, adopting a bit of Australian slang, may have
called the tune elsewhere, but not here.

To be sure, my first experience of public entertainment
was distinctly on the bland side, more edifying than
exciting. In the early 1920s my grandmother often took
me to the Monday "community nights" at the YMCA in

downtown Lancaster. The second-floor auditorium, entered past a man on a stool receiving free-will silver
offerings (a nickel wasn't silver, but it looked like it),
was ill ventilated and, when the windows on the Orange
Street side were open, noisy. The audience was composed
largely of school teachers, church ladies, and the sort of
men you might see at the Sunday afternoon religious
meetings in the same place.

First, we must get into the community spirit by singing. On the stage, a large white screen was suspended
from behind the proscenium arch, and at the appointed
time the lights would go off, one circuit at a time. The
master of ceremonies, a hearty middle-aged wholesale
grocery salesman named Bill Trost, came on stage, bearing under his arm a gleaming silver trumpet, and on the
screen appeared, as usual, the text of a song called
"Howdy Do." After lining out the first verse in his
serviceable baritone voice, Mr. Trost raised the trumpet
to his lips and accompanied the audience as they sang
the sprightly song. He never had to cajole, flatter, or
browbeat the singers; everybody joined in with great
good will.

Rapport having been established, the musical portion
of the entertainment followed. Many of the song slides
projected from the stereopticon in the balcony were
hand-made by a local artist whose capitals and lower-
case letters alike were simple and strong. I recall with
special admiration his flat-topped A's. The words only
were given; it was rightly assumed that the tunes were
familiar to all. We sang such imperishable favorites as

Stephen Foster's songs and popular pieces held over from the late war—"Keep the Home Fires Burning," "There's a Long, Long Trail a-Winding," and "Over There." In addition, we were kept abreast of the hit songs of the day. Even the corseted middle-aged teachers must have enjoyed belting out the chorus of "Mary Lou" and "When the Red-Red-Robin Comes Bob-Bob-Bobbin' Along," which remained in the Monday night repertory for years.

But it was the professionally made slides, sometimes containing the music as well as the words, that were the most artistic. The lettering, which was confined to the lower margin, was so precise that it must have been done by some mechanical process, but the greatest wonder was the colored scenes that illustrated every line, one dissolving into the next, smoothly and on cue from Bill Trost's tireless trumpet. "Oh, beautiful for spacious skies, For amber waves of grain," the song would begin, and behind the words appeared a richly colored scene featuring spacious skies and amber waves of grain, the kind of view that photographic-resource firms like Ewing Galloway supplied, in black and white, to the geography textbooks of the time. "For purple mountain's majesty, Above the fruited plain," the song would continue, and we would *see* the purple mountains and the fruited plain.

Finally the song session was over and Bill Trost bore his trumpet offstage. Some dignitary appeared to introduce the lecturer of the evening. A figure in a tuxedo came from behind the purple curtain at stage right, probably bumping into the protruding end of the pole

113

that weighted down the screen, and accepted the audience's applause.

> . . . and so let us begin our armchair journey tonight in the crowded harbor of Marseilles, where for miles and miles you see nothing but angled spars and masts, schooners and tramp steamers from every imaginable part of the world. On shore you hear a perfect babel of tongues, and the sidewalks are filled with swarthy lascars, cheerful Cockneys from London, Turks, Genoese, Australians, South Africans, sailors from every clime. We sail past the wharves of Marseilles, and within an hour or two . . .

At the exact strategic point in these preliminary remarks the lecturer pressed a button on the electric cord that led to earphones clamped on the head of the projector operator in the front of the balcony, and on the screen suddenly appeared Marseilles harbor in all its travelogue resplendence, painted ships upon a painted ocean, the swell of the waves seen from the prow of the lecturer's ship frozen in blue immobility. And we were on our way.

In the 1920s there was an abundance of travel lecturers. At any given time, it appears, half of them were in the field, toiling their way by caravan from Turkestan to Timbuctoo, or investigating, Sunday School anthropologists that they were, the more seemly traditions and customs of the African pigmies and photographing the more seemly aspects of their bodies. An equal number,

114

meanwhile, having exchanged pith helmets and parkas for civilized dinner jackets, were doing one-night stands on the provincial culture circuit. The monarch of the company, Burton Holmes, probably is the only one remembered today. He may have come to Lancaster once or twice, but I suspect his fee was out of the YMCA's range. One John C. Ostrander was more our style. It was an occasion for joy when, at the end of an evening, it was announced that our old friend John C. Ostrander would be with us next week, with a brand-new travelogue on the Pyrenees or the pampas. He came back with his pointer year after year, always with a fresh repertory of colored slides and pleasant anecdotes.

On deluxe occasions, we even had movies. At the end of a certain sequence of slides, the stereopticon operator would wave his arm in the beam of light suddenly issuing from the projection booth in the rear of the balcony, and on that cue, accompanied at first by an alarming spitting and hissing from the electric arc, there would be cast on the screen sweeping landscape panoramas or close-ups of wizened, tattooed natives of some South Sea island engaged in animated conversation or dancing to the beat of a tom-tom. (In those pre-Technicolor days some travel films were in sepia rather than black and white, so that even the lushest jungles had a sere and withered look.) This was years before movies "talked," so all we heard was the lecturer's voice, telling us what the dance was supposed to be and alerting us to watch the witch doctor in the middle.

One itinerant lecturer, however, went the Ostrander

115

set one better. His name was Branson Cou, and his specialty was not savage dances or statistics about the largest platinum mine in the world. Instead, he concentrated on the romantic, tranquil, reverie-inviting side of worldwide travel, showing us the most limpid lakes, the leafiest forest glens, the foamiest rapids; and to really put punch into his poetic script, he had an Orthophonic Victrola behind the screen, playing one record after another of the most atmospheric music that had yet been put on wax. The total effect of this early multi-media production was spellbinding.

Lancaster thus learned in public assembly what it was also learning at home, in the glossy-paged monthly issues of the *National Geographic*. There were, in both locales, vistas of the incredibly blue Mediterranean seen from some high point in Sardinia or Cyprus. There were scenes in oases and spas, in the Taj Mahal and the Alhambra. There were countless close-ups of laughing Swedish girls, laughing Dutch girls, laughing Borneo girls, laughing East Indian girls, laughing Eskimo girls, laughing Sudanese girls. In every well-regulated travelogue there was also a shot of a pouting child of one race or another, which could be depended on to arouse an affectionate little chuckle in the audience. There were pictures of mosques and Greek temples and French cathedrals and rude chapels in the Canadian Rockies; there were scenes in European capitals, the streets filled with pedaling cyclists, as motionless on the glass slide as a fly in amber; there were remarkable shots of somber-eyed tigers and leopards, taken at point-blank range.

About these latter achievements the lecturer always had thrilling tales to tell—how he had waited night after night, camera-trap baited, listening to the long-drawn-out yell of hyenas and the crackling and tumbling of the underbrush beneath the heavy tread of an elephant, but never any tigers until one night when . . .

> . . . but like all good things, our journey must come to an end. And as the sun slowly sinks into the Red Sea [this is not a parody: it is what we actually heard], and the spires and minarets of the ancient city gleam in the last rays, the time arrives to say goodbye to the haunting Orient as it settles down to another night of mysterious, brooding silence. It has been a genuine pleasure for me to be here with you, and I thank you for your kind attention.

The last slide faded from the screen, the lights came up, and we were back in the old-fashioned auditorium; there was our lecturer, his face bronzed and lined from the adventurous life, bowing graciously to our applause. We poured down the stairs and out into the autumnal chill of West Orange Street, never imagining that, long afterwards, our own county and the people we knew would become the subject of *National Geographic* picture stories.

Meanwhile, just around the corner from the YMCA, the second block of North Queen Street was becoming

117

Lancaster's Great White Way. Not that it boasted any Times Square-type signs advertising cigarettes or toothpaste; but it housed all of Lancaster's downtown movie theaters (there was one neighborhood second-run house that existed precariously on Manor Street), plus supporting establishments that made North Queen the city's central purveyor of spendthrift delight. Interspersed with the theaters were the drugstores I have already spoken of, and on the opposite (east) side of the street, two gleaming-white confectioneries, Miesse's and Sheetz's, with mirrored interiors, enticing window displays of filled candy boxes and sweet pastries, and lady clerks in immaculate uniforms presiding over the even more mouth-watering glass showcases.

The Scenic Theater, on the same side, was the oldest; its very name implied that it reached back to nickelodeon days, when the budding industry had to reassure nervous prospective customers that films, like spoken travelogues, were instructive as well as entertaining. Its screen was on the building's front wall, with the result that people coming in from the street while a show was in progress had to open the door beside it and so admit distracting daylight with every entrance. This was Lancaster's blood bucket, specializing in cheap thrillers and serialized Westerns. It quietly vanished sometime in the 1920s. Almost next door to it was a respectable house, the Grand, managed by a man named Bert Leighton, who wore a pince nez and loud suits and haberdashery that were a trifle ahead of, or anyway unharmonious with, the prevailing Lancaster fashion. He and his wife

118

were reputed to be retired vaudevillians, which could account for his taste in clothing, and for all I know, they were. Whereas the Scenic had a pianist to accompany the silent reels, the Grand had an organist.

Across the street from the Scenic and the Grand was the palatial Capitol. It occupied a site long dedicated to the movies, replacing the old Aldine, dating from the early days of D.W. Griffith if not still earlier, whose opportune destruction by fire enabled Lancaster to acquire a first-run house on the model of Philadelphia's magnificent Mastbaum, on Market Street opposite the "Chinese wall" on top of which the Pennsylvania trains arrived at Broad Street Station. Like many other cinematic temples of the era, the Capitol conformed to the Sam Goldwyn-Moorish style of theatrical interiors. The deep-piled carpeting and the subdued lighting in the lobby contributed to the half-reverential tone of the place; the hush was broken only by the distant murmur of the sound track behind the closed doors of the auditorium. To maintain the elegant effect, the management called the lobby the *foyer* and the balcony the *loge*. The rest rooms were *lounges*; a lighted sign over the men's showed a silhouette of a pipe-smoking man taking his ease in an armchair.

At the Capitol, indeed, the movie lover could enjoy every amenity that suggested itself to theatrical entrepreneurs and architects in the late 1920s. (It did, however, lack a ceiling depictive of twinkling stars and lazily floating clouds; for the summer-night sky effect, you had to go to the theater in Hershey.) There was a pit for the

119

orchestra which for a while accompanied the stage presentations, prior to the showing of the film, that were de rigueur in the metropolitan houses, not only the Mastbaum but, in New York, the Roxy and, at the end of the era, the Radio City Music Hall. Alongside the pit was the several-tiered console of the indispensable Wurlitzer, which was spotlighted when the organist, Ernie Stanziola, who will reappear later in this chapter, offered a medley of popular tunes to begin the program. I can date the Capitol's first season precisely: it was when "Valencia" was the hit of the year.

Two or three doors north of the Capitol was the Hamilton, under the same management but dedicated to second-run films and the occasional serial, this at Saturday morning shows for kids. Beyond that, at the corner of Queen and Chestnut, was the Colonial, the city's vaudeville house, a way station on the Keith-Albee circuit. The bill was the standard one for the time and place: a newsreel and perhaps a "short subject"—a travelogue or slapstick two-reeler—followed by five variety acts, a team of walking-stick-twirling hoofers in straw boaters and black-and-white shoes, even in the dead of winter; comedy skits, acrobats, animal acts, magicians, stand-up comedians, singing-sister duos, blackface turns, trick instrumentalists. These were accompanied, when required, by a pit band, whose leader, Joe Fratantuono, was ritually addressed across the footlights as "Professor." The show usually was continuous throughout the afternoon and evening, and latecomers could phase themselves into the action by following the printed program, which was cued to the letters of the alphabet, A to E, that appeared on lighted signs at each side of the stage.

I remember the asbestos curtain whose central landscape scene was surrounded by advertisements of local businesses, one of which, Lockman and Esches (I may not be getting the latter name right), regularly figured in the jokes and songs of comedians who tailored their material to the audience in any given city. The comic point about Lockman and Esches was that it ran a permanent going-out-of-business sale. Unfortunately, I recall nothing whatsoever about the names of the performers who came and went. My visits to the Colonial were infrequent, but on those golden occasions I must have seen a few of the vaudeville acts that later achieved fame on the Broadway stage and on the radio: Burns and Allen, Milton Berle, Bert Lahr, Jack Benny, Eddie Cantor, Fred Allen, Ed Wynn . . . Perhaps, in the memoirs of such veterans of the American variety theater, there are some indications of how the profession regarded Lancaster—the size and receptivity of the audiences it supplied, the hotels and restaurants they patronized during their stays, the ease with which the Pennsylvania Railroad enabled them to arrive and depart.

My chief recollection of the downtown theaters in general is of the ways in which they painlessly but dramatically taught me the difference between illusion and reality. I had an eye-opening experience one afternoon when I was sitting in the front row of the Colonial balcony, only a few seats removed from the spotlight operator. A conjurer was on stage, pulling off one amazing trick after another. At one point, he asked the audience to suggest something—a number, perhaps, or an object to be drawn from a hat or substituted for another that everyone saw had been stowed away in a chest. Without looking up from the magazine he was reading, the spotlight man called a number or named an object, which the magician instantly accepted as a "suggestion" and worked out the rest of the trick accordingly. This demonstration of blatant stoogism taught me, at an early age, that theatrical effects, however breathtaking, were not always on the level.

When the lights went up at the end of a matinee, the audience, still under the spell of what had occurred on the screen or behind the footlights, filed out of the lobby. Eyes that had been accustomed to darkness blinked at the sudden sunlight of late-afternoon Lancaster, where the sidewalks were crowded with shoppers and home-going workers and a procession of streetcars was about to divide itself to go in one of three directions, west or east on Chestnut or straight ahead on Queen. The memorable sensation of the moment lay in the psychic distance that separated us from the people on the sidewalk: they did not know, could not know, the pleasures of the artifice that had lately enveloped us. Alternatively, after the final show of the day at the Colonial, one could go through a side exit that opened directly onto the Chestnut Street sidewalk and find the street deserted and dark except for the street lamps, with only an occasional automobile or lonely streetcar in sight. Either way, the transition from Paramount or Keith-Albee theatricality to the commonplaces of the Lancaster scene was a momentary shock, like suddenly switching from warm to cold water in a shower.

There was also a lesson to be had in an alternative way of dividing time. As one emerged from the theater on the last evening of an engagement, the employees would be busy replacing the posters in the display cases on the lobby and outside walls and re-lettering the marquee. What had, until this moment, been an enticingly described and pictured "coming attraction" would, the next day, be the current one, to be featured at the entrance, and another film was accordingly announced inside. In the theater, the primary measure of time was the length of an engagement, sometimes complicated by a last-minute holdover that was officially said to be the result of unexpected popularity, but might also have been due to some trouble obtaining the already announced coming attraction. If memory serves, at one time, at least, the movie theater week began on Saturday, so that a new feature could initially enjoy the box office trade that was strongest on a weekend.

Two blocks away from the North Queen Street theatrical district was Lancaster's only legitimate theater apart from the vaudeville house, the Fulton Opera House on Prince Street, which had a plaster statue of Lancaster's first celebrity in a niche over the doors. Like many proper American heroes who enjoyed sculptural commemoration at the time, the inventor of the steamboat was clad in a toga. Built in the Civil War era, the Fulton had a good-sized main floor, a balcony, and a steeply raked gallery, or peanut heaven, which had the cheapest and hardest seats—benches, really—in the house. This was where traveling attractions other than vaudeville were booked. My mother often told me, and a newspaper clipping carefully preserved in a scrapbook I have lately found bears her out, that her sharpest disappointment as a young woman occurred sometime around 1906, when her husband-to-be had tickets for a performance of *Parsifal* at the Fulton, but they were prevented from going by a sudden snowstorm. The very idea of a touring Gurnemanz, Kundry, and Amfortas singing on a stage in the midst of the Pennsylvania Dutch country—on the site, moreover, of a jail where, as long ago as the 1760s, a Scottish Presbyterian gang of ruffians from up the Susquehanna who called themselves the Paxtang Boys had massacred a number of Indians being held there for their own protection—is as incongruous as Max Beerbohm's apparition at a Gulf gas station.

Road companies played the Fulton for runs of a week or so, and during several summers it had a resident stock company that offered everything from the classic mystery thrillers of the day, *The Cat and the Canary*, *The Ghost Train*, and *The Bat* to *Abie's Irish Rose*. This was where you could see the operettas whose music you knew from radio listening: *The Desert Song*, *Rio Rita*, *Rose Marie*, the perennial *Student Prince*. In the spring, local alumni clubs sponsored the appearance of student musicals, the Triangle Club from Princeton and the Mask

124

and Wig from the University of Pennsylvania. I saw them from peanut heaven, and still remember one line from the comic dialogue that I thought deliciously risqué: "Queen Elizabeth was the virgin queen; as a virgin, she was a success." (Or was it the other way round?)

Such little play-going as I enjoyed was usually thanks to a free ticket from one source or another. One indoor entertainment, however, was free to all, and when it was available, four times a year, I often took advantage of it; in the Depression years, one found amusement wherever one could. This series of unrehearsed dramas was staged in one of the auditorium-like rooms of the county court-house, which presided with all the majesty of the law over the intersection of King and Duke Streets. (The edifice was originally an example of Roman Revival architecture with steps as broad as the portico, but when the county offices it housed outgrew their space, frontal additions were thrust out on either side, narrowing the flight of steps and converting a classic building into something distinctly suggestive of the Sphinx.)

Here one watched the drama of criminal trials unfold. Most people in the audience doubtless had some personal interest in what was going on. As a mere idler, I had the luxury of complete detachment. Murder, manslaughter, felonious assault, and other violent crimes headed the bill, though this fare was varied by an occasional trial for such white-collar offenses as embezzlement, bribery, grand larceny, fraud, and (at least once) jury tampering. There was also a two-in-one felony called fornication and bastardy. This was the one sexual offense that was spelled out in the newspapers' lists of upcoming trials; others, including, I think, rape, were covered by the evasive designation of "serious charge."

These quarterly adjudications of Lancaster County's criminal activity had the same appeal that the Perry Mason detective novels were later to have: the suspense, the constant exposure of private lives and acts occurring in the very midst of the Lancaster one knew so well, the scraps between opposing counsel, the black-gowned judge in his swivelled, tilt-back easy chair, the sheer human interest of the ongoing drama without any hint of the outcome until the jury returned and the court official read out their verdict.

Among other things, I received a further lesson in the discrepancy between appearance and reality. Most witnesses were the sort of men and women to be met on Lancaster's streets and in its stores; they came to the witness stand in their own persons, fully recognizable. But some were not at all the same on-stage, as it were, as they were in their official roles outside the courtroom. These were the city policemen, township constables, and state troopers—the elite of Pennsylvania law enforcement officers—who took the stand early in the proceedings to depose to the circumstances of the crime and their subsequent part in bringing the accused before the bar of justice. Seldom, however, did they appear in the uniforms in which one was used to seeing them. Their civilian clothes, often so ill-fitting as to suggest they were bought off the rack at a cheap chain clothier's like Richman's, had the instant effect of reducing their stature, indeed demystifying them. Deprived of their uniform hats and badges in particular, they were stripped of their cachet of authority, reverting to the drab condition of ordinary men. There was something disappointingly reductive, too, in the matter-of-fact way in which they recited their testimony under the prompting of the examining attorney, as if they were wholly oblivious of the private misery in which they had become involved in the course of their duties.

What troubled me also was the seeming ambiguity of the law and the system of justice, and the arbitrariness of the rules that seemed to inhibit the discovery of truth. It was not so much that a defendant who had aroused my sympathy had failed to have the same effect on the jury that found him guilty or on the judge who sentenced him to a stretch in the state penitentiary. That was life, which had a way of undermining the way one saw things. But I became indignant when a pertinent question or a promising line of examination was abruptly cut off by the judge as he sustained the opposing lawyer's objection. It troubled me, too, to see some of the best minds of the local bar vigorously defending criminals who plainly deserved what the prosecuting attorney claimed they deserved.

I could not understand, either, how lawyers could so effortlessly exchange roles, a specialist in criminal defense turning up, after an election, as the new district attorney whose sworn duty was to prosecute the very sort of people that his former self had worked to have acquitted. A case in point was Charlie Eaby, a stocky courtroom star with crinkly, grizzled hair, whom I watched in action during many trials. Whether he represented the Commonwealth of Pennsylvania or sat at the other table, he had a tenacity, combined with a gift of sarcasm, that left me enthralled. I prize my memory of him as he sometimes concluded his grilling of a witness whose testimony, under his expert elicitation, had become more and more suspect. After a particularly egregious whopper, Charlie would turn to the jury and simply stare at it, his look saying more than could any words: "What do you think of *that* lie?" With that mute eloquence hanging in the air, he excused the witness or turned him over to the opposing counsel.

I must not give the impression that crime was especially rife in Lancaster. Although the Amish may have enacted dark deeds among themselves (in so tightly inbred a community, incest might well be suspected), neither they nor any other plain people were often involved with the law. They settled disputes among themselves, in their own way, and although they sometimes violated the law (their consciences forbade them to carry lights on their buggies, for example), they were seldom prosecuted. How law-abiding the city was was demonstrated by the fact that the police station was a little old building hidden away in a downtown alley, opposite the back doors where the East King Street stores received their consignments of merchandise.

My own contacts with the shady side of Lancaster life, outside the courtroom, were minimal. In the Watt and Shand delivery room there was easy talk of a downtown address where you would deliver a C.O.D. parcel and the "lady" who answered the door in a kimono would ask if you were disposed to take the bill out in trade; but this may have been sheer fiction. For some time, my idea of a "disorderly house," as the Pennsylvania legal lexicon called it, was simply a place where a drunken party got out of hand and the police had to be called. Once, my aunt's house on Wheatland Avenue was burglarized and for some reason I was deputed, as a fifteen-year-old, to act as her liaison with the police. In the course of our conversation, the state trooper in civilian clothes who came to investigate happened to mention the state of crime in the river town of Columbia. Buddy houses, he said, were numerous there. Since I knew that there was no college in Columbia, and therefore no fraternity houses or dorms, I was able to grasp that he meant something else. It was a nice instance of unintentional euphemism by mispronunciation.

Attending trials, I admit, was a rather specialized form of amusement, and I don't think many people shared my enthusiasm. Probably few of my contemporaries who became lawyers had ever been in a courtroom before they entered law school. Far more popular were the various outdoor entertainments that from time to time enlivened the generally staid atmosphere of the town. The circus—Sells Floto, or the amalgamated Ringling Brothers and Barnum and Bailey—unloaded its gaudily painted wagons from equally resplendent railroad cars on a siding and set up on a big lot called McGrann's

Park, which, like circus lots across the nation, was eventually built over. The parade, headed by a band followed by a succession of horse-drawn wild animal cages, several lumbering, slack-hided elephants, and mincing camels, wound up with a calliope and the indispensable ceremonial epilogue of an employee, sometimes in a clown suit, with broom and wheeled refuse can. No matter how familiar the sight, it never missed being greeted with a slightly embarrassed titter.

Patriotic holidays called for parades, especially on Memorial Day (sometimes called Decoration Day), in which grade school kids carried big bunches of peonies and iris, cut from flower beds at home, to one of Lancaster's several cemeteries. In open touring cars rode aging Civil War veterans wearing their distinctive slanted-front caps and a younger contingent of Spanish-American War veterans in the uniforms seen in photographs of Teddy Roosevelt and his Rough Riders.

Political campaigns sometimes were climaxed by election-eve processions, complete with bands, banners, and torches. I dimly recall watching one from a window on North Duke Street. Which election it was, I don't know; if it was for local offices, it may have been the occasion on which I added to my very young vocabulary the unusual word "coalition," because it was under that name that the Democrats (my father's party) and Republicans, or dissatisfied elements within the parties, following some now forgotten iniquities, put together a winning bipartisan reform ticket. Lancaster, both city and county, was usually conservative in politics, and its congressional district was always represented by a Republican.

For really big parades, marching bands were brought in from other towns, not only in the county but from as far away as Coatesville, Reading, Hershey, and Allentown. By an unwritten form of reciprocity, when out-of-town bands came to march in our parades, our own bands went to march in theirs. Perhaps this mutual-assistance arrangement extended to the hosts' social quarters. In long retrospect, it occurs to me that Lancaster's bands, the Iroquois, Elks, American Legion, and Knights of Malta among them, may have been dedicated less to a brassy St. Cecilia than to a boozy Bacchus, for in effect they constituted private clubs that were possibly less vulnerable than were profit-making dispensaries to raids during Prohibition and to liquor-law enforcement afterward. The most prominent feature of their rehearsal rooms was a bar, since beer was the best restorative for the body mechanisms that blew the horns, tootled the clarinets, and beat the bass drums.

The bands were part of a network of social organizations into which thousands of Lancastrians poured their energies and fraternal impulses. This network was dominated by the Rotary and Kiwanis Clubs, which flourished chiefly as a means of their members' forming useful business contacts at their weekly luncheons. Below these, there were numerous lodges and clubs, each with its own building or rented rooms: the Elks, the Moose, the American Legion, the Veterans of Foreign Wars, the Knights of Malta (and Pythias), the Masons, the Shri-

ners, the Odd Fellows, the Eagles, the Orioles, the Red
Men, the Patriotic Order of Sons of America . . . In
addition, there were the social adjuncts of the various
churches, sodalities and the Knights of Columbus for
the Catholics, the Epworth League for the Methodists,
Hadassah and B'nai Brith for the Jews. In the aggregate,
they satisfied for Lancastrians, as for urban Americans
countrywide, the gregarious impulse that Sinclair Lewis
found so ludicrous in the age of Babbitt and Dodsworth.

The bands often played, and some of the non-musical
organizations often picnicked, at one of Lancaster's two
amusement parks. Maple Grove, on the western outskirts
of the city where the Lincoln Highway crossed the Little
Conestoga Creek, may have been built to enrich the
revenues of the streetcar company, whose Columbia line
passed the entrance. Rocky Springs, on the other side of
town, was one of the many American amusement parks
that were put up at the very end of a trolley line which
had been purpose-built to serve it. They had in common
most of the major components of their kind: old trees
that could have benefited from dendrosurgical repair,
graveled paths, scruffy grass where there was any at all,
a swimming pool, a roller coaster, a shooting gallery, a
carousel (merry-go-round was the more usual word),
refreshment stands, a dance floor, a revolving swing with
cars in the form of one- or two-seat airplanes suspended
from it, and a dodgem (little cars, girdled with thick
rubber buffers, that derived their power from antenna-
like devices that scraped along an electrified metal ceil-

ing; the trick was to bump, or evade, other cars as their occupants steered them around).

Maple Grove had, in addition, a tunnel of love, an enclosed wooden watercourse activated by a stagily quaint water wheel, through which boats in the form of modified gondolas floated. The nominal attraction was the series of small lighted dioramas, sometimes static, sometimes moving, that were spaced along the pitch-dark voyage. The real attraction, as every teenage boy and girl knew, was the opportunity the darkness afforded for a quick smooch between pictures. There was also a so-called fun house, a not-for-the-claustrophobic firetrap, in which you groped through a labyrinth and were scared by a variety of crude visual and auditory ghost effects. Some of these properties might receive a fresh coat of garish paint every few years, but that was about it: the management probably saw no reason to maintain in tip-top shape attractions that were used only four months a year. Despite the splash of colored lights at night, when the tackiness was less evident, the total effect fell short of enchantment.

Both parks had a pervasive composite odor of roasted peanuts, caramel-coated popcorn, hot dogs, and the ozone that emanated from the dodgem's electric arrangements, as well as the localized smell of wet wool bathing suits in the swimming pool's changing rooms. They also had a dense medley of noises, the shouts and splashes of frolicking bathers, the gong at the top of the column at the try-your-strength (with a sledge hammer) concession, the thud of colliding dodgem cars, the pops of rifles at the shooting gallery, tinny tunes from the merry-go-round's mechanical organ with its cymbals and drums, and the fixed sequence of effects from the roller coaster: the clank-clank of the rack-and-pinion (or cogwheel?) mechanism that laboriously hauled the two-car train to each peak, followed by a tracking sound and the shrieks of the passengers as it plunged down into the abyss and then picked up momentum for the next ascent, whereupon the performance was repeated.

In an adjacent field, fireworks were set off on weekend nights, delayed noticeably beyond the fall of darkness so as to extort the most money from the crowd before the free entertainment began. Around ten o'clock there was a quarter-hour of noisy pyrotechnics so programmed that there was no mistaking the finale when it came, a climactic barrage in the sky or from a set piece on a figural frame. That was the signal for the appreciative honking of horns from cars in the parking lot, and the rest of the crowd made for the track where a caravan of trolleys waited to take them back to town.

Bordering on Rocky Springs was one of Lancaster's two public wooded areas, Williamson's Park, a touch of controlled wilderness through which the Conestoga Creek flowed. On the opposite edge of town, along the Harrisburg Pike, was Long's Park, which had winding roadways, mature landscaping, a picnic pavilion, and what can only be called a poor man's nine-hole golf course, no more of a challenge to irons, niblicks, or drivers than a croquet lawn. Both these and the amusement parks were favorite places to hold summer picnics,

134

whether small one-family or neighborhood affairs or church, lodge, or factory excursions or all-embracing family reunions that drew hundreds of people. Many came by trolley from as far away as the adjacent counties, and in the early years CTC freight cars, left over from the days when trolleys rather than trucks delivered merchandise to the outlying towns, arrived at the site, their floors packed solid with market baskets bulging with hearty food tucked in with clean white cloths. The pièce de résistance, apart from all the other Pennsylvania Dutch dishes, was "roastin' ears," freshly picked ears of sweet corn that would be roasted in an outdoor oven—the Lancastrian equivalent of baked clams on a Cape Cod beach—whose distinctive odor was that of charred husks. They were eaten with copious lashings of butter and salt. Afterwards, while the women cleared the long tables, there were pickup softball games and quoit pitching.

An occasional variant of the local mass picnic—I stress "occasion," because that is what it was—was a long summer day's excursion to Atlantic City to which a large local employer might treat his employees and their families. One such employer, Watt and Shand, closed the store for the day; a chartered train with a thousand or more men, women, and children aboard left Lancaster soon after dawn and arrived at the shore at mid-morning. When the returning train pulled into the station late that evening, the platform received a substantial number of cases of flaming, painful sunburn, upset stomachs, and general exhaustion. But by next summer, everybody would be ready to go to the shore again, at their generous employer's expense.

Except for high school and college football and basketball, organized spectator sports played little part in Lancaster life. In some seasons a lot with a single ramshackle grandstand called Stumpf's Field hosted a baseball team belonging to a *very* minor league, but it never put the city on the sports map. There was keener interest in the World Series, most of all when one of the Philadelphia teams, Connie Mack's Athletics or the Phillies, was playing. A big magnetic or mechanical diagram of the diamond, flanked by box scoreboards, was erected on the facade of the newspaper building just off the Square. Every play was reproduced on the diagram as it came over the wire, and the number cards slotted into the scoreboard were constantly changed according to the game's ongoing statistics. Additional information was provided by newspaper staffers shouting through megaphones. On a September afternoon, the crowds in front of 8 West King were so dense that police had to be stationed in the street to keep a lane open for the streetcars and automobiles to pass through.

While some Lancaster families went to the shore for their vacations, others drove up to cottages they owned at the little summer colony of Mount Gretna in Lebanon County. This was a form of going back to nature that was not much to my taste. Except for a swimming pool and a wooden auditorium that sometimes housed Chautauqua attractions or even a stock company that played selections from the Samuel French repertory of popular plays, there was not much entertainment, and while the small cottages had electricity, cooking was by kerosene, whose odor I always associated, unpleasantly, with the lack of creature comforts. I suppose it was good for people to "get away" for a while, but if I were pressed to choose—a contingency that happily never arose—I would unhesitatingly have preferred the paved streets and small amenities of city life.

For many modern Lancastrians, teenage and older, there was dancing. For private occasions, at the Country Club and elsewhere, Ira Bowman and His Orchestra, a band that was to Lancaster what Meyer Davis's several orchestras were to the haunts of the truly rich on Long Island and at Newport, provided a dependable evening's worth of fox trots and waltzes. The climactic event of the high school years was the prom, held an evening or two before commencement. Neither the boys' nor the girls' high school building had a gym suitable for dances—to have held them there, in any case, would have aroused memories of the daytime classroom that festoons of colored crepe paper would have done little to sweeten— and so a lodge hall, the Moose or the Odd Fellows, was rented. There the lights were low and the streamers looked a little more festive, particularly if a blue spot-light or two were added for romantic effect, and the cornmeal that was strewn on the floor made it adequately slippery.

Nationally famous dance bands seldom came to Lancaster. Regional outfits like Red Nichols and His Five Pennies were more the speed of the Rocky Springs and

Maple Grove "ballrooms" (to call them, more modestly, "dance pavilions" would have done those open-sided sheds ample justice). Name bands were familiar through their network broadcasts from fabled places like the Glen Island Casino and Frank Daley's Meadowbrook in the New York area and the Edgewater Beach Hotel in Chicago. There were bands for every taste, from Eddy Duchin, Hal Kemp, Nat Shilkret, Paul Whiteman, Guy Lombardo, Glen Gray, Henry Busse, and Fred Waring and His Pennsylvanians to the new-wave swing bands of the thirties, Benny Goodman, Duke Ellington, and Jimmie Lunceford, with George Olsen, Sammy Kaye, Jan Garber, and Glenn Miller scattered irregularly between. (The local equivalent of the day's novelty orchestras— Shep Fields and His Rippling Rhythm and Kay Kyser and His Kollege of Musical Knowledge—was an organization called Reg Kehoe and His All-Girl Marimba Band.) But these starry orchestras had to be sought elsewhere.

On summer evenings the Hershey Park Ballroom was the place to go, if one had a date and a car. This was where the big band era of the late 1930s was mostly celebrated; in tribute to which—and illogically, as far as I was concerned—most people didn't dance but stood in large, admiring knots in front of the platform. But that didn't matter; to be able to say that you'd "been to" Woody Herman or Artie Shaw was proof enough that you were in the mainstream of the younger set. Perhaps an even greater, though seldom voiced, satisfaction came from the sheer delight of walking with one's date at intermission through the Hershey Park gardens, the gravel paths damp and the shrubbery quietly dripping after a thundershower. At a certain age, this was the height of felicity.

It was not hard for a child to pick up a love of music in Lancaster. It was available on the radio, and in the 1920s it consisted largely of "salon" compositions played by a small ensemble such as one might hear at tea time in the palm court of a fashionable hotel, fluff like Ketèlbey's "In a Persian Market" and "In a Monastery Garden," the Berceuse from Godard's *Jocelyn*, Elgar's "Salut d'Amour," Rimsky-Korsakov's "Song of India," somebody's "Valse Bluette," and music from nineteenth-century French ballets. As time went on, there was a great deal of operetta music on the air. I heard so much Victor Herbert ("Kiss Me Again," "Ah, Sweet Mystery of Life," "March of the Toys," "Gypsy Love Song") that one of my earliest literary ambitions was to write a biography of him. I absorbed the facts of his life from whatever sources came to my attention: an Irishman by birth, a German-trained cellist, husband of an opera singer named Forster, subsequently an American citizen, musician in the Metropolitan Opera Orchestra, conductor of the Pittsburgh Symphony, and prolific composer whose name had been in lights on Broadway marquees year after year: *Mademoiselle Modiste*, *The Fortune Teller*, *Babes in Toyland*, *Naughty Marietta* . . .

A little later, the air waves were saturated with songs from the musicals of Rudolph Friml (*Rose Marie*, *The*

Vagabond King), Sigmund Romberg (*Blossom Time, The Desert Song, The New Moon, The Student Prince*), Jerome Kern (*Show Boat, Music in the Air, The Cat and the Fiddle, Roberta, Sweet Adeline*), George Gershwin (*Lady Be Good, Oh, Kay!, Strike Up the Band, Girl Crazy, Of Thee I Sing*), Rodgers and Hart (*Babes in Arms, The Connecticut Yankee, On Your Toes*), Cole Porter (*Anything Goes*), Vincent Youmans (*No! No! Nanette* and *Hit the Deck*), and Irving Berlin (*As Thousands Cheer*). Heard over and over again on the radio, songs like "Smoke Gets In Your Eyes," "Small Hotel," "Where Or When?," "I Told Every Little Star," "Lover, Come Back To Me,"—scores, indeed hundreds if you add the number of songs that originated independently of operetta and musical comedy—filled my repertory of effortlessly memorized lyrics. My memory of the words is sketchy now, but to borrow a line from a number called "The Song Is Ended," the melody lingers on.

There were also the light-classical repertories of radio orchestras like the Longines Symphonette and the Bell Telephone Hour orchestra. Complete symphony concerts could be heard once in a while but they began to be broadcast on a regular basis only toward the end of the 1930s. Meanwhile, I was exposed to whatever the public schools offered by way of musical education. When I was in grade school and junior high school in the 1920s, this took two forms as far as the ear of a prospective devotee of "serious" music was concerned. One was the broadcasts, for schoolroom consumption, of Walter Damrosch's Music Appreciation Hour, which ran for a number of years on NBC. I am afraid I associate no single composition specifically with Damrosch, his orchestra, and his painstaking explanations; only his avuncular German-tinged "Good afternoon, boys and girls" echoes in memory, and that doesn't get us very far.

The other contribution was a series of "Music Memory Contests" sponsored by local music stores (a later weekly contest show on the radio would be "Name That Tune!"). This involved listening in the classroom, for a period of several weeks, to a selection of compositions whose themes we had to commit to memory. I committed them so earnestly that I can recite a list today without book: "The Swan" from Saint-Saens' *Carnival of the Animals* as well as his "Danse Macabre," the sextet from Donizetti's *Lucia di Lammermoor*, Schumann's "Träumerei," the Largo from Handel's *Xerxes*, McDowell's "To a Wild Rose" and "To a Water Lily," Tchaikovsky's "Marche Slave" and "Andante Cantabile" (a movement from his string quartet in D major, but we were not told this), the "Dance of the Happy Spirits" from Gluck's *Orpheus*, Wagner's "Ride of the Valkyries" and the "Hymn to the Evening Star" from *Tannhäuser*, the movement of Haydn's "Surprise" Symphony where the sudden bang occurs. The idea was for us to identify each composition when it was played blind, as it were, in a formal competition. Under the tutelage of a sallow-complexioned fifth grade teacher named Euphemia Fassnacht, our class matched melody and title so accurately that one year we walked off with the grand prize, a state-of-the-art Ortho-

141

phonic Victrola, henceforth to stand in the front of the room to memorialize our prowess.

And so we acquired, if nothing else, a good basic repertory of names and melodies. This was augmented by the contents of the paperback books from which we sang once or twice a week: the intolerably sugary "Welcome, sweet springtime, we greet thee with song" (Anton Rubinstein's "Melody in F"), "Goin' Home" (Dvořák's New World Symphony), "Home to our mountains" (the Anvil Chorus from *Il Trovatore*), "Once more, dear home, we with . . . something, something [rapture?] . . . greet thee" (the Pilgrim's Chorus from *Tannhäuser*), "Glo-ry and [what?] to the men of old," whose second line ended with their . . . bold" (the Soldiers' Chorus from *Faust*).

Purists may deride this simple-minded introduction to something other than the popular sheet music of the time and the jazz band tunes that were deplored by people, music teachers among them, who subscribed to Walter Damrosch's standards of musical taste. It is certainly true that we missed even the most elementary analysis, of the sonata form, for example, or the rudiments of orchestral color. We were told nothing about the symphonic repertoire per se, and such small information as we possessed about operas understandably did not include the plots of *La Traviata* and *Tristan und Isolde*. But at the very least this kind of elementary musical education intimated that "good" music was to be respected, and that it was accessible in both meanings of the word.

There were recordings, even if they had to be turned over every three minutes, and there were also player piano rolls, their masters sometimes made by musicians of Rachmaninoff's stature, which even included punched performances of Italian operatic overtures (I recall *Semiramide* in particular) along with the more popular Victor Herbert medleys and Sousa marches. "Music appreciation" courses in schools and colleges have been much depreciated across the years, and no doubt many have been misconceived and even puerile. But all in all, the smattering of acquaintance I gained was not too bad a start for ears that eventually would be receptive to Bartók and Hindemith, which, along with Schoenberg, was as far as advanced musical taste anywhere extended by the early 1940s.

These kinds of exposure to music were available in any city the size of Lancaster, which had several thriving music stores that sold records, instruments and sheet music and had rooms in which private lessons were given. One, in addition, had a weak-voiced radio station that succumbed early on to its comparatively stronger competitor, and the other leading store—a son of the family went to Hollywood and gained fame as a songwriter with such pieces as "Daddy!"—had a small recital hall.

Lancaster also had the considerable advantage of being on the Community Concert circuit, the prime means by which live performances of serious music were brought to the nation at large. People subscribed to a series of four or five concerts a year, performed either at the Franklin and Marshall College auditorium or the

143

larger one at the new high school. By a reciprocal arrangement (parallel to, but not resembling, the one that existed between the parading bands), membership in the local series admitted one to Community Concerts anywhere else, so that Lancaster people could drive on other evenings to hear music at York, Harrisburg, Reading, even, for an especially celebrated attraction, as far as Allentown. In return for punching tickets at the door in Lancaster, I got a free season ticket for several years. My carefully preserved collection of programs is scarcely necessary to jog my memory: Lotte Lehmann, Helen Traubel, Rudolph Serkin, José Iturbi, Jascha Heifetz, Albert Spalding, Joseph Szigeti, the Busch Chamber Players, the Barrère Little Symphony, the duo pianists Bartlett and Robertson, the Cleveland, National, and Rochester symphonies . . .

Lancaster music lovers had the additional advantage of their proximity to Philadelphia, where they could hear the famous orchestra conducted by Leopold Stokowski. "Stokie" was then in the full flush of his colorful tenure and the scourge of the matinee subscribers who refused to hear the "modern" compositions he persisted in introducing and who, what is more, left early to catch the Paoli local that would deliver them to their Main Line homes before dinner. At the end of an evening concert at the Academy of Music it was just possible to hurry up Broad Street and catch the last train to Lancaster, the despairing, dying sounds of the last bars of the Pathétique Symphony still haunting one's ears. And once in a while a touring orchestra, not in the Community Concert series, came to town. One Sunday afternoon Nicholai Sokoloff conducted the New York Symphony, later to be merged with the New York Philharmonic, on the stage of the Colonial Theater, which was more accustomed to trained dog and comedy acts.

The music these orchestras played in Lancaster was identical with the programs they offered to other audiences when on tour. The repertory was strongly nineteenth-century Romantic. Beethoven, Schubert, Schumann, Mendelssohn, and I think to a lesser extent Brahms, were the meat-and-potatoes composers. Operatic overtures were almost obligatory—Weber's (*Oberon, Euryanthe, Der Freischütz*) and Wagner's (*The Flying Dutchman, Rienzi, Lohengrin, Die Meistersinger*)—but Berlioz was seldom heard. Mozart and Haydn, too, were still awaiting restoration to symphonic programs and Ravel and Debussy were on the fringes of acceptance, but Stravinsky and Bartók were far too advanced for concertgoers' tastes, at least in the provinces, and in any case they were still very much alive and continuing to compose. Symphonic programs belonged properly to the dead.

Organ recitals were common in Lancaster churches, and once, in Trinity Lutheran Church, I heard the town's leading piano teacher play the Beethoven Emperor Concerto accompanied by an organ reduction of the orchestral score. At Christmas and Easter there were seasonal oratorios, but only such standards, as they then were, as Stainer's *The Crucifixion*, Dubois' *Seven Last Words of Christ*, Gaul's *The Holy City*, and Men-

delssohn's *Elijah*. *Messiah* may have been sung sometimes, but it was far from being heard so often that it
became the over-welcome masterpiece that it is today.
Bach's cantatas went unperformed locally; for them,
and for the Passions and the B Minor Mass, one had to
go to the great springtime festival the Moravians put on
at Bethlehem. As for chamber music, it was never heard
on the radio and never played by local groups, in public
at any rate. As a child, I was taken once to a Sunday
evening concert by a Philadelphia string quartet in St.
John's Lutheran Church, and was so exquisitely bored
that my ears were closed to chamber music for many
years.

Ballets were a rarity. The Ballet Russe de Monte
Carlo, or one of its clones, turned up in one or two
Community Concert seasons, but the only performance
to make a deep impression on me was that of the Kurt
Jooss company from Switzerland, whose *Green Table*
ballet, a grotesque satire of fatuous, futile diplomacy
ending in the masked negotiators' shooting off cap pis-
tols, was frighteningly apt as war approached in Europe.

As I suggested when I mentioned the palm court music
issuing from the loudspeakers, radio came to Lancaster
early, and it helped break down whatever provincialism
lingered. One's sense of the larger world beyond southeastern Pennsylvania was enlarged by the very call letters
of the stations an Atwater Kent or Philco set pulled in,
especially on a cold winter night when distant reception
was at its best: KDKA Pittsburgh (the Westinghouse

station that was the parent of them all), WGY Schenectady (had anyone ever *heard* of Schenectady before General Electric built its powerful station there?), WBZ Springfield, Massachusetts, WMAQ, KYW, WLS, and WGN Chicago, WIP and WCAU Philadelphia, WRVA Richmond, WSB Atlanta, WHAS Louisville, WJR Detroit, KMOX St. Louis, WWL New Orleans, WOWO Fort Wayne, WHAM Rochester, WGR Buffalo . . . The very call letters were wrapped in the romance that Thomas Wolfe was meanwhile discovering in American place names. Some stations had particular associations. WPG Atlantic City ("*World's Play Ground*") had its studios on the Steel Pier, and on an excursion to the shore you could actually watch a broadcast through glass windows; if you were lucky, you could even see the station's Happiness Boys quartet (named for their sponsor, a brand of candy) harmonizing in person. WLW, Cincinnati's powerful clear-channel station that blanketed two-thirds of the country, won a permanent place in the affectionate reminiscence of youths on dates for its long-running Moon River program around midnight, a confection of mood-inducing verse read by a treacly voiced announcer alternating with suitably dreamy music from a theater organ.

Intercollegiate football in the days when Notre Dame and Army were the big teams became a national sport when NBC's Graham McNamee and CBS's Ted Husing were at their microphones in press boxes high above a packed, roaring stadium. Headline events gained incomparably in immediacy when Charles Lindbergh flew the

Atlantic and Lancaster neighbors working in their yards on that sunny May day in 1927 traded the latest news of his progress: WJZ New York said he'd been sighted by a steamer, WEAF, also New York, said he was over Ireland, WOR Newark, the voice of the Bamberger department store, said he was nearing Paris. The wonder of the dawning radio age, instantaneous communication outdoing the telegraph, was not readily downgraded into one of the unremarkable commonplaces of life.

Lancaster had a radio station of its own, actually one of the first in the nation. The prescient owners of the local newspapers had seen that sooner or later the new sound medium would join print as a popular means of information and entertainment, and they were determined to add it to their present monopoly, which they did. The station's call letters were WGAL, officially an acronym for "World's Gardens at Lancaster" but facetiously interpreted as "We Give Away Liquor." Its feeble power, one kilowatt, did not carry its signal much beyond the borders of Lancaster County, but it had an edge over many worthier stations in that it was allowed unlimited hours on the air, whereas they were "sundowners" that had to sign off at sunset so as not to interfere with the signal of distant stations on the same frequency. In addition, it was a network affiliate, carrying the programs of the NBC Red Network, whose key station, as anchors were then called, was WEAF New York. (The Blue Network, based at WJZ, later became the American Broadcasting Company, ABC.) Or, to put it more precisely, WGAL was a secondary affiliate. Instead of

148

broadcasting all the NBC programs available, it was allowed to carry some sustaining (non-commercial) shows in return for its availability when a sponsor wanted to piece out a larger network than usual.

WGAL operated on the fourth floor of the newspaper building at 8 West King. The studio appointments when I worked there in the middle and late 1930s did not, in any way, bear comparison with the shining new Radio City, NBC's New York headquarters. A long lobby, with worn carpeting, and dilapidated furniture acquired years ago by means of a due bill issued by a delinquent advertiser in lieu of cash, stretched the length of the suite. Facing it at one end was a control room with a high panel full of knobs and switches and meters, and a microphone for the announcer, who doubled as an untrained and unlicensed engineer. Alongside the control panel were a pair of turntables and a set of bins containing hundreds of worn pop records in a state of complete confusion. The two adjoining studios were acoustically treated with heavy drapes laden with dust that seemingly had accumulated ever since the station broadcast the Coolidge-Davis election returns in 1924. Studio A could accommodate a two-person interview or the daily devotions conducted by a "reverend" sent by the local ministerial association. Studio B had room for a six-piece band. If a broadcast involved forces that exceeded Studio B's modest capacity, such as the WPA concert orchestra which at one time rescued local musicians from the unemployment rolls, it had to be set up in the lobby, which had no acoustic treatment whatsoever and in

addition was within microphone pickup distance of ringing telephones and passersby at the far end of the room,
where, in default of private offices, we had our desks.

It was widely believed that the owners kept the station
on the air, by license from the Federal Communications
Commission, solely for the sake of occupying the frequency assigned to Lancaster and thus suppressing any
competition that might tend to draw off advertising
dollars from the newspapers. It was evident enough that
they couldn't care less about what went out over that
wave length from 7 a.m. to midnight each day. The only
steadfast listener was a paid one—Larry the transmitter
operator, a licensed radio engineer, who kept a lonely
vigil in his shed atop the building, at the foot of the
antenna tower that soared higher than the nearby Griest
Building. Except when "technical difficulties" put the
station off the air and he had to do what he could to put
it back, his only duty, hour by hour, day by day, was to
keep the log that the FCC required. In his cramped
quarters he had a Ping Pong table for the use of friends
who might climb up to him by the fire escape, and, being
something of a voyeur, he also kept a pair of binoculars
handy for solitary amusement. Up there on the roof, he
was in an unequaled position to see whatever of interest
was going on, publicly and privately, in a wide sweep of
downtown Lancaster.

The many gaps between NBC programming that came
off the long-distance telephone wire were filled locally,
by ordinary twelve-inch records and "electrical tran-
scriptions" (large 33 ⅓ r.p.m. recordings, lasting half

an hour, that were the precursors of the post-war LPs),
and by studio presentations. Among these were performances by the flotsam and jetsam of the Lancaster entertainment world. Once in a while the floor show of some
fly-by-night cabaret would come in en masse, the girls in
their patched costumes and the comic in blackface and
wildly checkered suit. Among the other luminaries was
an organization called the Susquehanna Mountaineers,
presided over by one Googie the Jugblower, a strange
being with prominent eyes and Adam's apple, who could
blow a jug with the best of them. An even stranger being
was Kayo Frankhouser, a stocky little man who seemingly made a living playing the piano in saloons. Once a
week, at the appointed hour, he would come into the
studio and wordlessly sit down at the untuned piano.
"Kayo Frankhouser," the announcer would tell the unseen audience, and without further comment Kayo would
launch into an uninterrupted program of jazz songs,
played by ear. At the end of fifteen (could it have been
thirty?) minutes the announcer would say "That was
Kayo Frankhouser," and Kayo would vanish as silently
as he had materialized.

Two men on our versatile staff had useful contacts
with Lancaster show business. One was Cliff Gray, a
darkly handsome announcer with a lady-killer moustache, whose more lucrative occupation was running a
picnic grounds-cum-show park somewhere in the back-
woods. Every Saturday afternoon during the season he
would help fill the broadcast day, and, not incidentally,
attract attention to his enterprise, by putting on a

hillbilly concert with himself as master of ceremonies. Years later, when Tennessee Ernie Ford became a star, I realized that he and Cliff were virtual twins, not only in their close physical resemblance but in their Southern mountain drawl and their partiality to country and western music. Cliff was the only true "personality" on the local radio scene.

Ernie Stanziola, a swart, cigar-smoking professional musician who came from somewhere up in the coal regions, had the official title of program director. In that capacity, he kept a scheduling board with seven long, parallel rows of hooks, each of which represented a fifteen-minute slice of the broadcast day, Monday through Sunday. On these hooks were colored tags specifying what particular kind of air-filler was to be broadcast at that time. Ideally, every segment of future time was filled comfortably in advance, but there were always a few tags marked "TBA" (to be announced). In the upshot, such intervals were filled by the *ad hoc* spinning of more records. Ernie's more important function, however, was to provide liaison between the management and the musicians' union, of which he was an officer. The station was not unionized, and so he was not, technically speaking, the shop steward, but he was a useful person for the owners to have around if any labor difficulties arose, such as a unionization campaign.

It will be gathered from what I have said so far that life at WGAL was characterized by a certain informality. Our motley group of factotums (in my case, combined continuity writer, studio engineer, announcer, receptionist, and whatever other roles were called for in emergencies) discharged our responsibilities confident that at any given time, except when we were safely on the network, our audience was neither large nor fastidious. Occasionally, when something had happened that brought the station to the edge of airborne anarchy, I inferentially dissociated myself from the mess by blurring our call letters: instead of WGAL, sharp-eared listeners might have heard something more like WBAL, which was the name of the perfectly respectable NBC affiliate in Baltimore. To my knowledge, nobody ever called this muffled disclaimer to the attention of either the management or the FCC.

At ten o'clock on weekday mornings, a full-figured secretary from Ephrata named Violet ("Tootie") Wechter came out from the newspaper publishers' executive suite to read the latest Department of Agriculture release in an endless series of "Household Hints" in her rich, natural Pennsylvania Dutch accent. For the length of time she was on the air from Studio A she was our resident home economics specialist. In an antic mood, we would make funny faces at her through the control room window, put up signs with rude sayings to further distract her, and even—this was Ernie at work—steal into the studio and tickle her. Somebody always was at the board, ready to switch off her mike if she broke up, but to her great credit she usually managed to preserve her aplomb.

If Ernie was not precisely the ringleader, he certainly set no example of discipline. If he suddenly tired of hearing a batch of records in their tattered jackets—the Dorsey Brothers, maybe, or Ted Fio Rito, or Ted Weems—he would gather them up and chuck them down the wastepaper chute. Wearing another of his hats, he was the official staff organist, though there was a difficulty here: we had no organ. He did, however, have access to the one at the Capitol Theater, where he was occasionally employed as *its* staff organist, and he scheduled himself for a half hour of "Morning Melodies" or some such title. Seating himself at the console some mornings, he would suddenly discover that his heart was not in his playing, and so he directed the engineer-announcer over the telephone line to put on a batch of records instead. Again, nobody objected to this deviation from the program announced in the newspapers to the point of telephoning in to complain.

Ill paid though I was, and however humble the station, I enjoyed the opportunity to realize an ambition I'd entertained ever since I decided that I wanted to become something other than a streetcar motorman. (This first, fervent ambition had faded as I came to understand that trolley driving offered little prospect of advancement; the highest you could go was to become a dispatcher who presided over the punctual movement of cars around the Square and sent off the last suburban runs at 11 o'clock each night.) I had no idea then that what I was called upon to do at WGAL had any bearing on my eventual, totally unforeseen, career as a university teacher. But, just as nature abhors a vacuum, so broadcasting abhors dead air, and it is an announcer's first duty to fill the wavelength with something, anything.

Ad libbing is also a talent indispensable to a lecturer who dislikes the cut-and-dried tyranny of prepared scripts. One day I interviewed a faded celebrity named Clarence Chamberlin, an old-time aviator who had followed Lindbergh across the Atlantic at a time when such feats still were headline news. He was now barnstorming the country in a clumsy old fourteen-passenger plane, and the interview was scheduled for half an hour; but after five minutes he dried up, and because it would have been too embarrassing, even in a station like ours, to fill the rest of the time with records, I had to keep the air filled with desperately contrived questions. Luckily, he could respond to my ad libs, albeit in a taciturn fashion, and we somehow kept going to the end of the half hour. In gratitude, he offered me a free sightseeing trip aboard his plane, and it was from that vantage point, standing behind him in the cockpit, that I first saw Lancaster from the air.

The station's manager, who was also its chief salesman, once sold fifteen minutes' time to a self-styled "Captain" So-and-So—I don't think it was Ahab—who had come into town with a dead whale on a railroad flatcar now parked on a downtown siding. Hauling around a portable microphone, I had to express suitable wonder at every aspect of this shabby embalmed denizen of the deep, and feed prepared questions to my host. (One question he warned me beforehand not to ask on the air concerned the nature of the long, large cylindrical object, also embalmed, that lay on the floor. He explained, sotto voce, that it had been an important appendage to the whale when alive). When the tour ended before the contracted-for time was up—there is just so much you can say about a dead whale—we adjourned to the reception chamber of the co-attraction, a headless woman, and I interviewed her.

The best preparation of all for a classroom career, however, was being color announcer on football broadcasts, for which there were no prepared scripts except for the commercials. WGAL became, for the occasion, the key station of the "Atlantic Refining Football Network," which consisted of a handful of other stations in eastern Pennsylvania and Delaware that were under the same ownership. We broadcast full seasons of Franklin and Marshall College football, both at home and away. At home we enjoyed the comfort of a section of the covered press box, but at one or two other colleges we had to make do with a place in the open stands, which presented obvious difficulties. Once a snowstorm forced us to contrive a makeshift radio booth from a large carton in whose lee the play-by-play announcer and I huddled for the duration of the game. On the other hand, after F & M played Fordham on Rikers Island, New York, and I had treated our listeners to copious descriptions of the metropolitan skyline, the suddenly generous management splurged and stood us, the crew, to drinks and dinner at the Café Rouge of the Hotel Pennsylvania, with Benny Goodman's orchestra on the bandstand. This was the broadcasting business at its most sybaritic.

Radio announcing supplied another valuable spin-off for the future teacher-lecturer, a precise sense of timing. However loosely organized the proceedings in the studio itself may have been, as network broadcasters we were slaves of the clock. NBC's ritual "bong-*bong*-bong" at ten seconds before the hour was a signal to all stations along the line, rousing their inattentive or dozing microphone-tenders to remind them that the local air was theirs for the next minute, for station identification and maybe a commercial or a time check. Having constantly to keep the eye on the clock, so that I would be ready to "climb off" and "climb on" the network according to NBC timing, doubtless contributed to one professional skill I later sought to cultivate, the pacing which enabled me, admittedly for effect, to finish a classroom lecture precisely at the moment the bell rang.

I cannot say that writing continuity (i.e., spot commercials) did anything to evoke or improve whatever facility of language I may have possessed. I once prepared a spot advertising a set of "beautiful blue-green blown beverage glasses" that a store had on sale. It was our regrettable habit not to look at copy before airing it, and on this occasion Cliff Gray, who was the victim, returned it to me, the offending tongue-twisting words underlined and a big "what the hell?" scrawled in the margin. I understood what he meant. On one memorable day the station manager, seeking to win over a Dodge dealer by giving him a "courtesy sample," had us play

157

eight recorded commercials, supplied by Dodge's national advertising agency, back to back. At some time or other I was required to compose a *five-minute* commercial in favor of—I forget what it advertised: a shoe repair shop? an auto parts store? a pawnbroker? In any case, I threw conciseness to the winds and composed and delivered a veritable treatise in as persuasive language as I could muster. I doubt, though, that it brought a noticeably enlarged stream of customers through the advertiser's doors.

It must be added that we treated the news with a modicum of restraint. To be sure, there were mornings when I had to open the station with a newscast only to discover that Jasper, the night janitor, had forgotten to turn on the teletype machine; but this was an easily remediable crisis, because I had only to go downstairs to get a copy of the morning *Intelligencer-Journal*. But once the teletype was chattering away in its closet across from the control room, WGAL kept its audience informed of world events, and my proudest day as a radio journalist came in December 1936, when I shuttled between the machine and the control room microphone with the latest flashes on the abdication of Edward VIII. Mere election nights, when the management went so far as to bring ham sandwiches and coffee to our returns-strewn table, didn't compare with this vicarious participation in world events.

These pages on life at a "coffeepot" (low power) radio station are my small contribution to a colorful chapter in American social history between the two World Wars that has yet to be written, and perhaps never will be. All the existing histories of American broadcasting concentrate on the networks and a few big-city stations, and even within this restricted compass they say little about the informal operating side of the industry—the personalities and careers of the announcers, the programming, the unscripted incidents, all the material of the kind that has been amassed and preserved in, say, the many histories of American railroading. There is a fair amount in print, though it is not easily found, on the humors and crises of small-town journalism, but there is no such body of recorded lore about its electronic sibling.

I have far from exhausted the anecdotes my memory stored up during my menial stint in radio. Some of my WGAL colleagues have even gone unmentioned—Eddie, the only man among us with the exception of Larry at the transmitter and his relief man, Bill, who knew an ohm from an ampere; Dave, the sports announcer whose unquenchable enthusiasm for athletics that ranged from the PGA Masters' Tournament to a local sand lot team, was to keep him at the station, and eventually its TV sister operation, throughout his working life; and Bill, the engineer who reluctantly doubled as an announcer in a pinch and whose voice when before a microphone compulsively converted every declarative sentence into a question, like this? I don't know how many old-timers survive. But their dwindling number is all the more reason for arrangements to be made for them to contribute their memories to an oral history project. Local broadcasting played an important role in American popular culture, and the inside story of its early years should be placed on the historical record while there is still time.

LEARNING

Lancaster had as good a notion of what was going on in the world as any city of the time was likely to possess. Most middle-class homes had their assortment of magazines: *Collier's*, *Liberty*, the *Reader's Digest*, the *Saturday Evening Post*, *Red Book*, *Cosmopolitan*, the *American* (filled with business success stories), *Good Housekeeping*, *Ladies' Home Journal*, the *Woman's Home Companion*, the *National Geographic*, even *Judge* and *College Humor*, the prime jazz-and-flapper-age weeklies with drawings by John Held, Jr., and humorous pieces by S.J. Perelman. The *Saturday Review of Literature*, *Harper's*, and the *Atlantic Monthly* found their way into a few high-middlebrow homes, and I presume that the *Nation* and the *New Republic* were available at the public library. The big innovations in the thirties were the Luce publications, *Time* with its idiosyncratic prose, *Life* (soon imitated by *Look*) with its exciting and informative picture spreads, and the expensive and opulent *Fortune* for Lancaster's few tycoons. *Esquire* was deemed, on the whole, a bit too racy for Lancaster subscribers, though they could buy it at newsstands.

The Philadelphia dailies, the *Inquirer*, *Bulletin*, *Record*, and *Public Ledger* arrived every day (the latter two folded sometime in my childhood), and the *New York Times* was delivered on Sundays. These supplemented the national and world news printed by the local papers, all three owned by the same family that kept WGAL on the air. The afternoon *New Era* was, for its time and place, a well-edited paper; its politics were unswervingly Republican, and its leading syndicated columnist was the Hearst papers' Arthur Brisbane. The morning *Intelligencer-Journal*, product of a merger that occurred before my time, was for the most part a warmed-over version of the previous day's *New Era*. To provide a semblance of balance, its politics were perfunctorily Democratic, which did the owners no harm when that party took over Washington in 1933. The *Sunday News* ran some features and had a reasonably good comic section.

None of these papers were inclined to rock the boat. They gave their readers a selective account of what went on in town, their editors responsive to the expressed interests of the publishers and advertisers. Except when a scandal broke so publicly that it could not be ignored, such as a sitting judge's extra-legal affair with a woman attorney who practiced in his court or an embezzlement case involving a prominent church-going banker who was caught with his hand in the till, the definition of news that was fit to print was constricted, but no more so, I imagine, than in most cities. Muckraking, to be called investigative journalism when it once more dominated the headlines in the 1970s, was simply not the Lancaster style. In this respect, the Lancaster papers were unaffected by the example being set across the river, where the feisty editor of the York daily, one Josiah Gitt, persisted in making waves.

The *New Era* was edited primarily for city circulation, while the *Intell* (for short) had more news and features of interest to country readers. In town, they were distributed by carrier boys with their canvas bags; along the country trolley lines, the motorman hurled wrapped copies out the open door as the car sped on, trusting they would land in the approximate vicinity of the subscriber's front yard. As a service to downtown passersby, late news bulletins, copied with a broad black pencil on big sheets of newsprint, were posted in a glass case at the entrance to the newspaper building.

Like all newspapers that subscribed to the wire services, the Lancaster ones reciprocated with local stories as required. Once in a while their reporters filed dispatches about major crimes or wrecks to be picked up by other papers in the region, particularly those in Philadelphia, to which Lancaster stood in the relation of a familiar hinterland. Lancaster hit the Philadelphia headlines when, in an isolated outcropping of the gangsterism that accompanied Prohibition, somebody picked up a city police lieutenant named Gainer on West King Street and took him for a ride, in the then customary sense of the term. What happened after that remained a

163

mystery for some days, until his body was found in the Philadelphia papers' own circulation area, the Main Line town of Ardmore.

Before Prohibition, Lancaster had supported several breweries, which duly submitted to padlocking when the eighteenth amendment became law. One of these was Rieker's, whose premises lay behind Mr. Stapf's butcher shop, at the point where West King Street turned into Columbia Avenue. Some years later, Federal agents seem to have had reason to keep an eye on the premises. To their bafflement, they noticed an occasional truck making a delivery of something or other and then coming away empty. It took much patient surveillance and sleuthing to solve the riddle. Someone, quite possibly one of the city's out-of-work brewmasters, had had the brilliant idea of committing to Rieker's vats the supplies the trucks had brought in, obtaining a satisfactory product, and then conveying it through the municipal sewers in old fire hoses, emerging at some distant point, perhaps another "closed" brewery, from which it was distributed to thirsty southeastern Pennsylvania.

The wire services out of Lancaster carried stories every February describing the Groundhog Day ritual at Quarryville, when a group of ceremonially decorated citizens gravely pronounced whether or not a—I suppose hypothetical—groundhog saw his shadow on warily emerging from hibernation, which was the clue to whether or not six more weeks of winter lay ahead. This non-event was, however, overshadowed by the much better publicized version at Punxsutawney, in the central part of the state. (Among the Amish a holiday, which they were reputed to spend fishing, was St. Swithin's day, 15 July; they had somehow got hold of the English proverb that if it rained on that day, it would rain for forty days thereafter.)

It was Lancaster's reporters, too, who first notified the world of the goldfish-swallowing contest at Franklin and Marshall's fraternities, a craze that spread to the entire nation's campuses. I do not remember what record was set—it involved the number of fish swallowed in a given number of minutes—nor do I remember which election year it was when Franklin D. Roosevelt's campaign train stopped in Lancaster. It was not much of a story, least of all for those of us who had waited more or less impatiently from twilight well into the evening for the much-delayed train and whose memories of the occasion would be limited to the image of a far-off rosy blur on the platform of the observation car. That was all we saw of the president, and only the next morning's paper would tell us what he said.

One event that acquired *ex post facto* importance was the arrival in the sky over Lancaster, one quiet twilight in 1927, of the *Shenandoah*, a long silver cigar-shaped dirigible (the cigar analogy was inescapable). It moved so quietly, even at a low altitude, that it was only by accident that I, walking along Columbia Avenue near the brewery, happened to look up—and there it was. The largely unnoticed visit would have merited only a paragraph or two in the next day's papers, except that early that morning the giant airship ran into bad weather somewhere over Ohio and crashed, killing all who were aboard.

One feature I remember in the *New Era* was somewhat off the beaten journalistic path: boiler-plate serial fiction in which the syndicator left blanks to be filled with local references—places, stores, institutions, even the names of prominent citizens for walk-on characters. There was no better way of introducing verisimilitude into newspaper fiction, and since none of the real people named had anything to do with the plot, which was enacted by people with fictitious names, there was no danger of a lawsuit.

One of the staples of the *New Era*, less so of the *Intell* with its country circulation, was the social page, which chronicled every Lancaster wedding, club meeting, and dance that was brought to the paper's notice, as well as more private events—a family going on vacation, out-of-town guests arriving, students leaving for college or returning from it, birthday parties, luncheons and bridge parties held—complete with the names of all the persons present. It was axiomatic then that the more personal names appeared on the social page, the more readers the paper had. Gathering such news was usually the work of a woman on the staff, but on the *New Era* there was a reporter who was out of the ordinary: a blind, and I think partially paralyzed, middle-aged man named Ovid Musselman, who spent his days in a darkened apartment on Vine Street telephoning people to ask for their "personals," which his devoted wife, much younger then he, would type up and deliver to the office.

No name occurred more frequently in those columns than that of Mrs. Albert M. Herr, the very model of a civic leader, who seemingly had her finger in every pie. She was the wife of a wholesale florist who was known to the local scene only as the husband of Mrs. Albert M. Herr. There was not a club or a cause—all of them respectable, of course—of which she was not at one time or other an officer, and when not an officer she was still a leading light. She was nonetheless never a socialite who hobnobbed with the local elite for the cachet involved, and I think she never dabbled in politics. But she was an indefatigable and generous person, and though it was possible to smile at her sheer ubiquitous visibility in Lancaster, I remember with gratitude her giving me the Community Concert ticket that exposed me to so much good music at an impressionable age.

Mrs. Herr was the archetypal club woman at a time when Main Street and Gopher Prairie overflowed with them, much to the amusement or outright disgust of the iconoclastic writers in the *American Mercury*. They did cut foolish figures, but at the same time they made their communities just a little less philistine than they would otherwise have been. The culture they aspired to may have been a poor thing, but it was better than nothing. Lancaster may have been a slightly stonier seed ground than most cities of its size because of the puritanical influence wielded, however indirectly, by the conservative churches. It was not a question of expressed antipathy or suppression so much as one of indifference: a significant part of the middle-class community simply was not interested in secular culture. And yet, under these discouraging conditions, it was still possible to acquire a certain amount of humane culture.

In addition to the book departments and lending libraries at the two stationery stores, Ream's and Herr's, there was a full-fledged bookshop on West Orange Street, owned by a notorious grouch named Hervey Hurst. Since I had no money for books and Hurst did not encourage browsing, I cannot say whether or not it was a good bookstore.

The public library was on North Duke Street, opposite a heavy granite structure that housed the city post office before it moved to larger, up-to-date quarters elsewhere. The library was not an especially inviting place; it was furnished in dark wood, the lighting was poor, and the facilities for sitting down and having a happy read *in situ* were on the austere side. The establishment was supported, in a fashion, by income from various legacies as well as small token payments from the city and county treasuries. It could not afford to plug the leaks in the roof, let alone buy more than a scattering of new books. The cultural statesmen of the town, a pathetically small lot who nevertheless kept doggedly trying to improve things, sought one means after another of getting a library of which at least a town half Lancaster's size would not be ashamed. As a last resort, they proposed that the city itself support the library out of tax revenues. The question was put on the ballot, a big campaign was waged, and the voters spoke, with a resounding No. Lancaster was justifiably proud of its low tax rate.

Still, I never lacked for books to take home. It was among those shelves that I first contracted the bibliophilia that was to influence, if not determine, my professional career. It began with an adolescent passion for the writings of Christopher Morley, his personal essays and his once popular book, *The Haunted Bookshop*, whose central character was a gentle, pipe-smoking bookseller with a temperament the very opposite of Hervey Hurst's. From these I proceeded to the whole current literature of book loving and book collecting, mainly in the form of essays by such living contemporaries as Edmund Lester Pearson and A.E. Newton. I once saw Newton plain—the Philadelphia manufacturer of electric circuit-breakers whose *The Amenities of Book Collecting* did more in its time to popularize that hitherto recondite hobby than the less well known causeries of other rich bookmen. I was on a train from Lancaster to Philadelphia, and he got on at Daylesford, the station just east of Paoli that was named for the nearby estate where he communed with his precious first editions and association copies. I recognized him from the hound's-tooth suit he wore in one of his photographs, and it made my day. This was my first contact, however casual and momentary, with bibliophilia in the flesh.

I do not think many people were then aware of what I see in retrospect as a yawning gap in Lancaster's culture at that time. Such books on art as the public library contained may have been relatively up to date, but the reproductions were in sepia or black and white, faithful color reproductions then being beyond the reach of the existing technology. One had to go to Philadelphia, to the massive new Parthenon-like structure dominating the far end of the Parkway that Thomas Craven once called a "Greek garage," or to the Pennsylvania Academy not far away, to see original art of whatever age or school. Lancaster had no public, or even private, collection; the few paintings in private hands were family portraits from the easels of such artists of limited fame as Gilbert Stuart's pupil Jacob Eichholtz. Only late in the 1930s was there heartening assurance that better times were coming, when issue after issue of *Life* featured full-color reproductions of selected Italian masterpieces and lesser works of art then in fashion, especially the paintings of contemporary Americans, Grant Wood, Edward Hopper, Thomas Hart Benton, John Sloan. One carefully detached these full-page pictures from the magazine and saved them; even more than phonograph records, they brought a welcome smattering of current culture into ordinary Lancaster homes.

Public education in Lancaster was probably no better and no worse than elsewhere. The conventional subjects were taught, from first grade to senior year in high school. If there were outside pressures, political, social, or what not, that decisively affected what or how we were taught, I was unaware of them. The curricula for college preparatory and "commercial" students in high school were basically prescribed, though there was some choice in electives. The college prep subjects were heavy on information (English, history, foreign languages, math, science), the commercial ones on skills, such as typing, shorthand, and bookkeeping. Teachers had a clearly defined job to do, and they did it to the best of their ability and the degree of their patience and commitment. As everywhere, there were good teachers and bad ones.

In my years, the high schools, on the edge of downtown, were still segregated by sex (the old word for gender). The Boys' High School, consisting of two floors of classrooms enclosing an auditorium on the main floor, with a gym in the basement, and Stevens (girls') High were two blocks apart. There was increasing traffic between the two, because coeducation was being gingerly introduced by the exchange of classes, so that students could take courses not given in their headquarters building. In the mid-thirties the two schools were merged in a new, completely coed plant in another part of town. Having graduated by that time, I was deprived of the luxuries, as they rightly seemed, of McCaskey High.

The most lasting memories we accumulated of our classroom days centered as much on our teachers' idiosyncrasies as on the question of how effective or ineffective they were in ensuring that we left the room each day a little better educated than we had been fifty minutes earlier. Every American high school of Lancaster's size must have had as wide an assortment of teachers who were memorable for one reason or another, and so ours may well be regarded as typical.

One of the English teachers had a classroom manner

that can best be described as evangelical, doing a selling job on a pantheon of nineteenth-century American authors ranging from Edgar Allan Poe, Henry Thoreau, and William Cullen Bryant to FitzGreene Halleck, Charles Fenno Hoffman, and Joseph Rodman Drake. We wrote down all the names as he wrote them on the blackboard, along with his enthusiastic comments. I think that, even then, I was a bit skeptical of the latter three: were they really as important as Poe and Thoreau? This suspicious eclecticism worried me until I learned more about American literature in college and discovered that Halleck et al. were small fry indeed, compared, say, with Melville and Emily Dickinson. Why, then, did F.J. Heckman clutter his course with them? A little later, the answer dawned on me: he had taken summer courses at Penn State, where one of the pioneers of American literary history, Fred Lewis Pattee, had been teaching for many years. Pattee was as big on Halleck et al. as he was on their greater contemporaries (he had, indeed, momentarily rescued them from total oblivion), and what we dutifully took down from F.J. Heckman, Heckman had earlier dutifully taken down from F.L. Pattee. I have never read a page of Halleck or anyone else of that ilk, nor have I ever felt a compulsion to do so; but the episode casts a rather interesting light on the way American education worked, and to some extent still does.

The French teacher, far from being a blackboard evangelist, adopted what we were ready to believe was the sophisticated classroom manner. William Atchley, slim, of medium height, and dapper, was, to us, the epitome of suavity. His boulevardier mannerisms, as we took them to be, impressed us as being not so much affectations as natural extensions of the subject he taught. He also played tennis, which nobody else on the faculty did. He and F.J. Heckman seemed to have little in common—many years later, they might have been described as an odd couple—but outside school hours they were close associates. Such was the state of my innocence, if not my classmates', that I deduced nothing scandalous from that fact. Had I done so, I might well have been wrong.

Next door to the French classroom was one presided over, in a fashion, by William Armstrong, an English teacher who was universally called Army, though never to his face. He was a curious being, stocky, with tight curly blond hair and a light complexion, who was given to sudden, uncontrollable rages. If a student proposed a wrong answer to one of his questions or committed some small delinquency, he would fly off the handle—and then, painfully gaining control of himself, he would come to the student's desk and nuzzle him, whether with accompanying terms of endearment or not, I, perhaps fortunately, don't recall. The story was that he had been shell-shocked in the war, but whatever the origin of his hang-up was, to have him as a teacher day after day was a little unsettling.

The most honored teacher, in terms of student respect, was a red-moustached, nasal-voiced exponent of history named Monroe Sloyer. He was reasonably demanding; in fact, there was no nonsense about him, though he kept his temper and was never deemed unfair. I learned, then, the standard accolade that a bunch of adolescents could bestow on a teacher who was no patsy, knew his stuff and taught it well. In fact, said the consensus, he shouldn't be wasted in a high school: he should be a college prof. Although nobody invoked a specific contrast, one was at hand. Another social studies teacher was the football coach, who, in accordance with practice then and now, had to teach at least one class in an academic subject. His Red Tornado team won some and lost some; I doubt if it ever had a protracted winning streak. What I do remember is that he was as bored as his classes, and pronounced the famous economic doctrine "lazy fare."

The math teachers were a mixed bag. All I remember of one is that he sported a little Charlie Chaplin moustache. Another, who unfortunately had to bend over me pretty often to correct a calculation, had a bad breath that in those days went by the name of halitosis, a Madison Avenue coinage that did wonders for the sale of Listerine. A third earned our respect, in a different way from Monroe Sloyer, by being known to moonlight in striped shirt and black pants and sneakers, a whistle on a cord around his neck, as a basketball referee. This was one way of making the extra money that ill-paid teachers had to resort to. Fred Rentz, who periodically stuck a pencil in his ear and taught German and Latin— his trick was to refer us, offhand, to the exact number of the relevant section of the Latin grammar—was an ordained Reformed minister and supplied the pulpit in country churches. Another Latin teacher could be seen on Saturdays astride a salesman's fitting stool in Kinney's shoe store. I wonder if he was as embarrassed as I was: somehow it seemed below the dignity of an academic to sell shoes, or anything else.

Brief glimpses of teachers' private lives, including their struggle to support a family, were inevitable in Lancaster. A music teacher at the girls' high school bore a hyphenated name, the sign that she was a divorcée: a rare bird in the community at the time, and an even rarer one in a school. She was an object of covert curiosity, though I doubt if anybody learned anything more about divorce in general than they did about hers in particular. A retired principal of the high school was once picked up for driving "while under the influence," but I don't think he lost any standing in the community as a result. No one acquainted with the difficulties of school administration even in those relatively uncomplicated times would have begrudged him his drink at the Elks' Club.

When they were ready for college, and could afford to go in Depression days, Lancaster's youth had ample choice. With good academic credentials, they might go to either of the two famous liberal arts colleges on the outskirts of Philadelphia, Haverford or Swarthmore. If, in addition, their families were well heeled they might go, perhaps by way of the Hill School or Lawrenceville Academy, to an Ivy League school such as Harvard, Princeton, or the University of Pennsylvania. Their sisters likewise might attend one of the Seven Sisters—Bryn Mawr, Mount Holyoke, Vassar, Wellesley. . . . It was, however, only the exceptional scion of a Lancaster family who aimed that high. Far more went to colleges affiliated with their religious denominations, none more than a few hours' drive away: Gettysburg, Wilson, Muhlenberg, Ursinus, Dickinson, Hood, Cedar Crest. Penn State offered the advantage of low tuition for students living within the borders of the Commonwealth. At a pinch, one could commute by trolley to the Millersville State Normal School, one of the chain of public teacher training institutions whose academic pretensions were minimal. The day was not foreseen when the whole system would be upgraded by legislative fiat to "universities," demonstrating once more that in America it was the name, not the thing, that counted.

But the college that attracted most men students from the city and a few from the county was only a mile from the Square by trolley or foot. Franklin and Marshall was a church-related college, and as such might have—and in some ways did—fit the stereotype of such small institutions nationwide, over which hung a persistent aura of intellectual mediocrity and an outdated ethos. They were off the pace that marked the best colleges of the time, which may have meant simply that they clung to more of the past than they should have. Franklin and Marshall's mandolin club, which had come and gone in the 1920s, still was listed in the catalogue in 1940. But as I look back I detect numerous signs of the college's breaking out of its mold, a slow process constantly marked by an

176

ambivalence that had considerable impact on the community at large.

Like most such institutions, it served a regional clientele, mostly from Pennsylvania and Maryland but also including an increasing number of students from New York City's suburbs and New Jersey, who were popularly believed to be Ivy League rejects. Its historical affiliation was with the Reformed denomination, whose theological seminary was across the street. But those ties were weakening, whether because the financial support the church gave to the college was diminishing or because the college, for its part, was deliberately assuming a posture of independence I do not know: probably both. Money was increasingly coming from private donors who may or may not have been members of the church. Chapel attendance was no longer compulsory and there was a fair representation of national fraternities. The college's traditional mission of preparing young men to be ministers, lawyers, teachers, and, in general, unremarkable but sturdy pillars of the communities to which they returned after four years (or, for Lancaster residents, in which they remained) was broadening. A growing number of graduates were becoming scientists, and thanks to unusually good departments of biology and chemistry, Franklin and Marshall was coming to be known for the excellence of its pre-med training, which practically guaranteed that its alumni would be accepted by the best medical schools.

The college was one of the strongest links Lancaster had with the past. Franklin College had been founded in

1787, the year the Constitution was adopted; one of its sponsors was Benjamin Franklin. Marshall College originally was located in the hills of central Pennsylvania, in the town of Mercersburg. The two were merged before the Civil War, Marshall College bringing its Reformed Church affiliation with it, and the resulting institution settled on a large plot in northwestern Lancaster. Throughout its subsequent history it had the distinction of being one of the few campuses in the nation not bisected by a road or a city street. Its original trio of dark red brick buildings, the obligatory Old Main with its equally obligatory chapel, and the matching Goethean and Diagnothian debating society halls (probably inspired by Princeton's Clio and Whig) that flanked it, as well as many old shade trees, tied the campus to the 1850s. In the period between the World Wars, a spate of new buildings—dorms, library, gym, swimming pool, labs, classroom buildings, auditorium—were all built in the colonial style of lighter red brick with white trim that tied it more visibly to the Philadelphia of Benjamin Franklin's day.

The town-gown relations between Lancaster and its resident college were just about average for the time, part affection and part distrust. Students and faculty, it was agreed, were good for the local economy, including the sector that rented out rooms and supplied the dorms and fraternity houses, and the college's presence unquestionably added to the city's prestige as a good place to live. Some college events engaged the community, such as the pajama parades downtown that were for a while part of the freshman initiation routine when the hapless "frosh" with their little blue beanies ("dinks") were urged by the sophomores, wielding paddles, to climb lamp posts and blow out the electric lights. In the absence of any but the most minor-league of baseball teams, the city's athletic interest centered on Franklin and Marshall football. On pleasant late afternoons in the autumn, the blue-and-white-shirted "gridders" having posted a victory, the Old Main bell pealed out and the satisfied crowds streamed from Williamson Field onto College Avenue, where smouldering piles of fallen leaves along the curbs gave off their aromatic smoke and a line of trolley cars waited to take people downtown.

On the other hand, there were "those fraternities," whose position in a society as conservative as Lancaster's was always shaky. The brothers did not always maintain the best relations with their neighbors along West James Street and College Avenue, and they sometimes threw riotous parties at which, with the end of Prohibition, beer was on tap. Fraternities played a prominent role in the lives of Lancaster's datable young women: you were socially handicapped if you were not invited to their parties, but disturbing stories were told about the goings-on that involved injudicious intakes of beer and giddy, complaisant girls.

Moreover, the prevailing assumption in Lancaster held that the professors, some of them anyway, were a radical and/or agnostic lot—a presumption that floated in the town-gown lore of innumerable American communities with something of the force that imputations of "secular humanism" have today. It was certainly true that a significant number of professors did not go to church. This unease was mitigated to some degree by a few public-spirited professors' participation in certifiably respectable activities, hobnobbing with businessmen in Kiwanis and Rotary and engaging in good works at large. One of the more controversial of the latter was the co-op grocery set up by a few avant-garde faculty members and their wives, collaborating with like-minded outsiders from places like the Unitarian Church. The ideals behind this project were undoubtedly high, but so were the prices. The middleman, it is true, was eliminated, as were the profits, but the A & P and Acme chains, buying in quantity, could undersell the co-op any day of the week. It never flourished.

Faculty members were generally admired as repositories of recondite information if not necessarily wisdom. It was a symptom of this respect, as well as a token of the outside world's ignorance of academic distinctions, that they were spoken of or addressed, interchangeably, as "professors," a title most could legitimately claim, and "doctors," which many could not, the M.A. then being a sufficient proof of intellectual superiority for its bearer to hold a college job. None of the non-Ph.D.s, so far as I noticed, ever disclaimed the doctorate with which the common parlance endowed them.

The highest level on which Town met Gown was the monthly meetings of the Cliosophic Society, Lancaster's top cultural symposium. Town dressed up for the occasion, dinner jackets for the men, long dresses for the women, in order to show it was well disposed toward the values represented by Gown. The two groups more or less alternated in reading papers that had something to do with the arts or literature, and presumably Town felt better for its brief excursions into the realms of gold.

Relations between the college and the community were further enhanced by the availability of men in the business administration and scientific departments to serve as consultants to local firms. Several "doctors" were in great demand for talks before civic groups. Their doyen was the longtime chairman of the history department, a white-haired gentleman whose distinguished bearing, which combined affability with an air of authority, made him the very archetype of the locally venerated sage; I venture to suppose that there was one such, at that time, in every small college in the land. Great though the demand for him on the ladies' afternoon club and men's service club circuits was, he struck me as being less successful as a teacher. When I took his course in English history, a subject indispensable to an English literature major, we were required to read the standard textbook, which is where I learned all I got to know about English history at that point. His class meetings were given over, for the most part, to informal commentary on the foreign news in yesterday's *New York Times*. "Boys," I remember him saying when the Italians conquered Ethiopia, "I want you to watch these developments closely."

Nowhere was the ambivalence that I now realize marked the college in those years better exemplified than

181

in the chairman of the religion department, who was also the minister of St. Peter's Reformed Church at College and Buchanan Avenues, the nearest the college came to having a campus church. As theology then went, Charlie Spotts was a liberal. He spoke well of Reinhold Niebuhr, tended not to worry about the literal inspiration of the Bible, and was committed to the proposition that the church should have a social mission. He set up, for our virtual idolization, the then prevailing sainted image of Albert Schweitzer, the world's greatest exponent of Bach's music, whose sacrificial service to humanity consisted of his setting up and running a hospital in the depths of the African jungle.

That was one side of Charlie. The other I glimpsed only once, I think, and that by accident, but the moment ineradicably engraved itself in my mind. It was a gloomy, gray Monday morning, and in his office Charlie was receiving a report on Lancaster's weekend iniquities, a blue movie shown at some lodge's stag party, perhaps, or a girlie magazine on surreptitious sale at a news dealer's, or something that was not quite right at a fraternity party. The man who conferred with him was the sort for whom the word "gumshoe" must have been invented: gray in face and garb, he exuded distaste for his occupation as a paid snoop. I had earlier seen a similar revulsion in the face and manner of a physician whom the state board of health routinely sent to high school assemblies to deliver frank man-to-boy lectures on the dangers of venereal disease. (Perhaps put off by his dreary delivery, I failed to make a mental note of anything he said.) The glum gumshoe's services were underwritten by the local Law and Order Society, headed at that time by the longtime rector of the (high) Episcopalian church, a clergyman named Twombly who enjoyed great prestige in Lancaster. I do not know how Charlie reconciled in his own mind what seemed to me to be antithetical positions, outspoken liberalism in churchly matters and blue-nosed moral policing in secular life.

I was never aware of any overt suppression of opinion at the college. There must have been unspoken limitations on what a faculty member could say on the economic and political issues that were coming to the surface in the first New Deal years, but Franklin and Marshall was probably under no more restraints than most institutions, and in fact may have been luckier than most. The concept of academic freedom was hardly recognized simply because no one, including several young Ph.D.s from major eastern universities who had recently joined the faculty, was disposed to make an issue of it. There was, however, the hovering presence of Henning W. Prentis, Jr., who combined the three potent roles of president of Armstrong Cork, the city's biggest industry, president of the National Association of Manufacturers, and— president of the college's board of trustees. It was an explosive mixture, but it never ignited. The fact remained, and everyone was aware of it, that the governance of the college resided ultimately in the hands of the man who, as the head of the N.A.M., was the implacable mouthpiece of entrenched conservatism, an economic royalist or an industrial statesman, depending on your point of view.

My commitment to the principles embodied in the Rooseveltian New Deal had its origin to some extent in certain classrooms at Franklin and Marshall, but chiefly in the conversations of faculty members who belonged to an extra-curricular offshoot of the English department. The Calumet Club was an invitational paper-reading group composed of students, not all of whom were English majors, and faculty, not all of whom were from the English department: there were professors of French, psychology, mathematics, and sociology as well. We met in the faculty members' homes, and after a paper was read by either a student or a teacher, we adjourned to the dining room for a buffet supper provided by the host. The dean of the college happened to be a member of the English department and his regular remark as we passed around the table and filled our plates, "This is a veritable repast!", was not far from the truth. It was at his house, if I am not mistaken, that beer (beer!) was first served at a Calumet meeting: a daring innovation at the time, but rendered wholly licit not only because Prohibition had been repealed but because a dean has prerogatives not always vouchsafed to lesser men.

For a small liberal arts college only gradually emerging from the constraints of its religious affiliation, Calumet was a rather extraordinary group. Darrell Larsen was the profane, cigarette-addicted, and passionately dedicated director of the Green Room Club, which luxuriated in a professionally equipped bijou theater that was

184

part of the liberal arts building. He prepared more than one alumnus for the Broadway stage, and another for an Oscar-winning directorship in Hollywood. In later years, after his time, Green Room graduates were to star in films and television. He once put on a production of *The Duchess of Malfi* that was featured in *Time* magazine.

Darrell had only a B.A., which was adequate for his specialty, but the other men in the English department contingent, all but two of them young, had Ph.D.s from Johns Hopkins, Princeton (two), Harvard, and Pennsylvania. One was to go from F & M to become editor of the Benjamin Rush papers at Princeton and later was editor-in-chief of the great edition of the Adams family papers at Harvard. Another would become a professor of medieval literature and linguistics at Brown. A third went to another eastern university as professor of philosophy and fell victim to McCarthyism in the 1950s. Their intellects and talents were passed on to the next generation. One son, a baby then, would become a Harvard Ph.D. in Chinese studies and reopen the *New York Times* bureau in Peking after its long closure. Another would blossom into a prominent Broadway scene designer. And a third became Princeton's greatest basketball star before Bill Bradley, swept the university's academic honors, after military service wrote a doctoral dissertation on Milton, and then served many years as the president of a leading midwestern college.

The undergraduates didn't do so badly, either. In my time, they included a future career officer in the foreign service who would end up as the ambassador to Cambodia at the height of the Vietnam conflict, a dreamer of impossible literary dreams who would write a number of books, and one of our generation's leading sociologists. At least three others went on to receive Ph.D.s in English at Princeton, and still others won doctorates in psychology, chemistry, and French. Thrust into the midst of this coterie of eager and ambitious fellow-students and sharply intelligent teachers, one could not help learning. Since the faculty members were more or less self-selected, and they in turn selected their most promising students, the talk that went on over the plates of fruit salad smothered in whipped cream and cups of coffee made Calumet meetings the most liberal (in the sense of mind-freeing) part of our undergraduate education. I imagine that none of us thought, at the time, of the kerosene-lit Amish farmhouses a few miles down the Old Philadelphia Pike, from which no one ever went to high school, let alone college; where government, if it impinged at all on life, was distrusted and kept at bay; where secular books were never seen; where there was no formal art but only decorated domestic artifacts, and no music except the unaccompanied hymns of seventeenth-century German pietism. To live in Lancaster was to live in the midst of polarities.

Epilogue

If this book had been written in a contentious spirit, its
epilogue might have been titled "The Rape of the Garden
Spot." What happened to Lancaster city in the decades
following the hasty installation of the sentry box in
Buchanan Park was not unusual: it was a paradigm of
what happened then to hundreds of American cities and
towns. But the fate of the plain people's county was
scarcely paralleled elsewhere. The folk cultures of the
Appalachians and the Indian southwest were lamentably
exploited, to be sure, but for sheer intensity and ruth-
lessness the packaging and marketing of "the Pennsylvania Dutch country" was unmatched.

The city suffered a severe blow just after the war when
Park City, one of the largest enclosed malls at a time
when this revolution in American merchandising was just
getting under way, was built on farmland just west of
Long's Park. Its effect on the old downtown shopping
district was immediate and ruinous. (Watt and Shand's
shrewdly hedged its bets by occupying one of the anchor

stores, the other being Gimbel's, out of Philadelphia and New York. The owners of Hager's, the other leading department store, were less foresighted and within a few years their building opposite the Central Market stood vacant.) Both sides of the second block of North Queen Street, including all the movie theaters and the drug stores and confectionery shops, were torn down, and, in a misbegotten attempt at "urban renewal," a patch of brutal concrete "public space" was created at the corner of Queen and Chestnut and new buildings erected around it. The biggest was occupied by a new department store, an offshoot of an old-established one in Allentown, which hung on for a year or two and then closed its doors. On several other sites ugly multi-story parking garages were constructed.

Elsewhere within the now antiquated city limits, many landmarks, including the homes of some well-known families and scores of modest home-owned businesses, were demolished, and their quiet neighborhoods pock-marked with fast food stands, convenience stores, drive-in dry cleaners, cheap little "taxpayer" shopping strips, and branch banks. The city's building and zoning codes were no more restrictive than they had been, and in a time of headlong entrepreneurship they were powerless, as they stood, to stem the tide of so-called modernization that transformed the former inoffensiveness of the urban scene to sheer tawdriness. The loss was by no means offset by the efforts of a belated preservation-and-restoration movement.

In the surrounding townships whole complexes of

residential neighborhoods sprang up between the old "pikes" that radiated out in all directions, and along with them ancillary shopping centers and supermarkets with their acres of blacktop paved over the fertile farming soil. Here and there new industries—a big printing plant on the site of the county fairgrounds, factories making such disparate products as electric razors and outboard motors—appeared. A returned native, who once had easily carried a detailed map of the territory in his head, would find himself lost at every turning or new traffic light. Familiar street names no longer matched their surroundings, and new ones were no help at all. The Manheim Pike outside northwest Lancaster, a traffic artery congested with both local traffic and traffic from the Pennsylvania Turnpike in one direction and the newly built Lincoln Highway bypass in another, became a metallic jungle of used car lots, truck terminals, warehouses, and similar undecorative enterprises. The same transformation took place, on a reduced but still drastic scale, outside every country town. Once these had typically consisted of a single main street, several blocks long, and a number of shorter intersecting streets that ended in fields. Now they were surrounded by suburban sprawl in the form of jerry-built tract housing.

Route 30 from York to Lancaster was rerouted, to cross the Susquehanna on a new bridge north of the old one and then strike across the countryside, once the site of Mennonite farms, that was swiftly obliterated by big motels, industries, and Lancaster's western suburbs, where it turned into a bypass that eventually flowed onto the old road several miles east of the city. From there, it became a corridor lined for miles by "resort" hotels complete with all kinds of recreational facilities, manufacturers' discount outlets, souvenir shops, billboards advertising a "working Amish farm" that was open to the sightseeing public, a fifty-four-acre Dutch Wonderland amusement park, complete (God save the mark!) with a wax museum depicting local history, and every other kind of tourist trap that ingenious imaginations, prompted by avarice, could devise. It was on this sleazy stretch of highway east of Lancaster that the degradation of Lancaster County could be seen in its most concentrated form.

This was not wholly a post-war development. As early as the 1920s Lancaster was dimly conscious of the economic potential of tourism. The presence of the Amish farmers with their "quaint" customs, dress, and language in the "gently rolling" countryside was noted, along with the city's role in the founding of the nation and its thriving industries, in the pamphlets the Chamber of Commerce circulated. When state conventions were held in town, the attendants might be taken on a sightseeing tour by chartered streetcar.

In the thirties, stimulated by the outburst of regional interest that was part of the general resurgence of pride in things American, people discovered that the Pennsylvania Dutch had a long tradition of native applied art and decoration, notably in the *fraktur* work on samplers and such documents as birth certificates, and the big eastern museums and private collectors scoured Lancaster County for outstanding examples; the results of their searches would eventually be displayed in the American section of the Metropolitan Museum of Art and the Winterthur Museum of Colonial Americana in Delaware, among other places. Journalists got wind of this discovery and wrote articles about the Pennsylvania Dutch and what they were like. Photographers from national magazines traveled the back roads and snapped the Amish unawares; no matter that being photographed was against their religion.

Pennsylvania Dutch crafts and souvenirs began to appear in local gift shops, including the one in the German Village bus terminal, where the murals in the restaurant and cocktail lounge had appropriate themes. East of town, on the Lincoln Highway and the "Old Philadelphia Pike" (State Route 23, which was the original Lancaster-Philadelphia road) appeared restaurants advertising Pennsylvania Dutch food. The first orange-roofed Howard Johnson's in the area served no regional dishes alongside the chain's famous fried clams and twenty-eight flavors of ice cream, but it was called "the Amish Village" just the same. Local companies ran bus tours, and one could even see rubberneck wagons, as tour buses used to be called, with out-of-state, principally New York, license plates. At least one of my high school teachers and one of the professors at Franklin and Marshall rode them as guide-lecturers.

Compared with what was to come, however, the Lancaster tourist trade was not excessive, and although vulgarization was already setting in, it was not so blatant as to arouse much protest; the county setting and its people's settled, simple way of life, not to mention their privacy and dignity, were not imminently threatened. But something happened in the 1940s, and I wonder if it was not the local drum beaters' realization that not much could be done with that other selling point, Lancaster's supposedly distinguished past. It was a case of trying to make bricks without straw. Except for the single day when the Continental Congress, feeling the hot breath of the British army as it threatened to march up the Philadelphia Pike, sat in the Lancaster city hall in the middle of Penn Square only to decide that it had better put the Susquehanna between it and its pursuers, no nationally memorable events had taken place in Lancaster County. The age of several downtown stores was no more exciting, in itself, than the statistical fact that Lancaster had been the biggest inland city in the new republic.

Nor was the local hagiography very usable, when you looked closely at it. Although Robert Fulton may or may not have devised a manually operated paddle-wheel boat when he went fishing on the Conestoga, he left Lancaster for Philadelphia when he was seventeen, and he launched his steamboat on the Hudson, not the unnavigable Susquehanna. Benjamin West, born indubitably in Chester County, spent only a year in Lancaster as a young man, during which time he painted portraits of several local eminences.

If Lancaster could boast that one of its citizens, General Edward Hand, was a signer of the Declaration of Independence, two other associations the city had with the Revolution had a contrary aura of betrayal. Peggy Shippen, granddaughter of one of Lancaster's most revered and patriotic elders, married Benedict Arnold, and Major John André, the cultivated young British staff officer who was later to be hanged at Washington's headquarters for his involvement in Arnold's conspiracy at West Point, spent part of an earlier captivity in Lancaster as a parolee in the household of a solid citizen named Caleb Cope. James Buchanan's presidency was not much to celebrate, and possibly his greatest distinction was that he was the only unmarried American president. Thaddeus Stevens was remembered only for his involvement in the grimy politics of the carpetbagging Reconstruction era, especially as a prime mover in the impeachment of Andrew Johnson. As for literary celebrities, while Amherst had its Emily Dickinson and Hannibal its Mark Twain, the best Lancaster had done in a literary way was to witness the birth and death, at Columbia, of Lloyd Mifflin, whose only claim to remembrance was that he wrote nothing but sonnets. (He had died as recently as 1915, at his home Norwood, which would later become a Catholic convent.)

Lancaster, moreover, had no monuments or shrines to attract tourists at a time when Marion, Ohio, was building an imposing classical tomb for Warren G. Harding. It had no neighborhood preserved intact from colonial days, such as Philadelphia's Elfreth's Alley with its cobblestones and vintage house- and shop-fronts; nor, for that matter, was it even in the running when

Philadelphia could boast of Independence Hall with its treasured Liberty Bell, Carpenter's Hall, Betsy Ross's house, and any number of other buildings intimately associated with the nation's founding. Only because of the paucity of more interesting landmarks did the promotional literature cite the Ten Hour House on South Prince Street, whose construction from cellar to roof in a single day in the 1870s won a bet a sporting businessman had with wiseacres who maintained that it couldn't be done. There was a battlefield east of Lancaster but considerably nearer Philadelphia—Brandywine Creek—to say nothing of Valley Forge itself, and to the west, three or four hours by car on the Lincoln Highway, lay Gettysburg. But nowhere in Lancaster County was there an expanse of hallowed land to attract the interest of the National Park Service.

So, as competition for the tourist's dollar was becoming ever more feverish, Lancaster could not get much mileage from its history. But the county had an unsurpassable natural resource in its plain people, who, to put it crudely, proved to be Lancaster's ace in the hole. Beginning in the late 1940s, the Pennsylvania Dutch craze took off. A Broadway comedy hit, *Papa Is All*, made a travesty of Amish life. (The very title was a travesty. It meant "Papa is dead," but the expression actually applied to food or other commodities, as in "The shoofly pie is all," i.e., all gone.) The play, regrettably, entered the summer stock and amateur repertory and was sometimes chosen for high school performance.

A few years later the allegedly "rollicking" musical

comedy *Plain and Fancy* ran for more than a year on Broadway, and Eddie Fisher's recording of the song "Young and Foolish" was one of the day's top hits. The show had none of the ingratiating flavor of, say, its predecessor *Oklahoma!*, which did not exploit anything, since its setting drew on a widely distributed, not narrowly specific, society. *Oklahoma!* was not quaint; the Broadway "Amish" productions were predicated on a factitious quaintness that offended everyone who knew what the plain people were really like. More recently, the film *Witness* brought the Amish to additional millions of people, but this time, with the exception of a most unlikely affair between the hiding Philadelphia detective and the improbably sexy daughter of the family, the Amish theme was treated with relative respect and fidelity. Its unfortunate effect, however, was to increase still more the flood of sightseers, a busload of whom figured briefly but authentically in the picture.

Fatefully, the popularity of *Papa Is All* and *Plain and Fancy* coincided with the completion of the Pennsylvania Turnpike, which delivered the tourist traffic from metropolitan New York, in particular, to the Amish country in a matter of hours, using one of the exits in the Welsh Mountains or farther west, at Ephrata or Lebanon. The exploitation then shifted into high gear. Hokum, kitsch, schlock, and sleaze—call it what you will—took over as the already famous hex signs became the glibly promoted symbol of all that was meretricious. In such places as home-beautiful magazines and *New York Times Sunday*

Magazine appeared advertisements for everything from ashtrays to cocktail napkins with hex signs.

Once I even saw along the highway a sign advertising "Dutch soda," whatever that was. "Dutch" was the magic word that could be applied to every kind of food or artifact for which a market could conceivably be created. As far afield as George Town, Grand Cayman Island, I recently ran across a prominently displayed rack of saffron-colored cellophane packets bearing, surrounded by hex signs, the imitation-*fraktur* legend "Pennsylvania Dutch candy." The lollipops, caramels, and sour balls they contained had no possible Pennsylvania Dutch connection, and some were, in fact, marked "Product of Holland." All that was authentic was the distributor's 17-thousand zip code, which placed him within reasonable distance of Pennsylvania Dutch country.

In the countless souvenir shops in the region could be bought "gifts" ranging from books and pamphlets on (mostly bogus) Pennsylvania customs and lore and slews of Amish cookbooks to dressed Amish dolls and ceramic or wooden plaques bearing quaint dialect "sayings" that purported to spring from the wisdom of the folk. Pennsylvania crafts were available in suspicious abundance. Such cottage industries as quilt making—genuine Amish quilts became collectors' items and are now displayed in leading museums—gave way to enterprises whose connection with cottages (read "farm houses" in this context) was hard to discern. At the bottom end of the line were Amish joke books and ribald postcards with a

Pennsylvania Dutch angle whose full effect could not be achieved unless they bore the postmark of Intercourse (zip 17534), a village in the very heart of Amishland. In the 1950s the publisher of an allegedly pornographic magazine swelled the post office's revenues and over-taxed its limited resources by mailing entire issues from there.

When a railroad museum was built at Strasburg, south of the serried ranks of tourist traps along Route 30, half-hour steam train excursions, using old Pennsy rolling stock, were initiated on an authentically old branch that connected with the main line a few miles away. Situated in a field midway was a farmer (true Amish or an impostor, like the young women in Amish costume who now stood behind some counters in the Lancaster mar-ket?) who drove his plow up and down as long as he was visible from the train, after which he supposedly rested, on museum company time, until the next scheduled load of gawpers passed by.

When the once lightly traveled back roads and the newly created parking lots in the little towns became congested with buses and private cars, the plain people, Amish and Mennonites alike, found their traditional way of life was irreparably disrupted. Amishmen coming to auction sales found themselves on display before throngs of curiosity seekers. Publicity, uninvited, intrusive, in-escapable, destroyed the privacy they had always taken for granted—they can hardly be said to have "prized it," because it had never been seriously threatened before—as Pennsylvania Dutch land became a highly

197

promoted attraction for multitudes of Americans and, as my encounter with the Swiss woman proved, foreigners as well: five million a year, all told, according to a widely circulated estimate. Probably the ubiquitous Japanese, cameras at the ready, have swarmed from the buses in the last few years. I have not inquired.

Transformed from self-effacing, self-sufficient people into money-making curiosities, the plain people faced a dilemma: fight them, or join them? There was another alternative, of which a small number of Amish took advantage. They sold their farms (reputedly at huge prices, so valuable was the land for non-agricultural purposes) and moved away, to the Midwest or elsewhere. The rest remained, stubbornly clinging to the old ways and avoiding, so far as was humanly possible, contaminating contact with "the world." Some left the land to become valued construction workers, locally and in the Philadelphia suburbs. A few, like the proprietors of the pay-as-you-enter Amish farm, turned entrepreneurs in their own right. The Mennonites, who had successful businessmen and bankers among them, saw no harm in making an honest dollar and set up their own souvenir shops and dining places. They represented the most authentic element in the garish world of Pennsylvania Dutch commercialism.

No group seems to have put up strong resistance to the encroaching exploitation, or at least none succeeded. Although a few renegade Amish and Mennonites helped the process along once it started, the onus of guilt lies elsewhere, and there is plenty to go around. It is impossible to determine how much of the impulse to exploit the Pennsylvania Dutch scene on a grand scale came from within the Lancaster community, and how much from outside. Probably it was a combination of both, each accommodating, working with, the other, most of the initiative and timely assistance coming from within Lancaster, and much of the capital from outside. Certainly no community like Lancaster, however high-minded, could have wholly resisted the temptation to make money from so rich and available an indigenous resource. But just as certainly, no would-be profiteers from outside could have imposed their will absolutely on the people involved; in the phrase that probably entered the language about the time the wholesale vulgarization and commercialization began, it took two to tango. I suspect that some of my Lancaster contemporaries and their children have done very well for themselves in one or another of the numerous tourism-related businesses. I wonder if any of them have ever paused to consider what they have done to the place where they grew up.